THE ZODIAC KILLER

By Carla Mooney

Content Consultant
Duffy Jennings
Journalist and Author
Formerly of the *San Francisco Chronicle*

AMERICAN CRIME STORIES

Essential Library
An Imprint of Abdo Publishing | abdobooks.com

ABDOBOOKS.COM

Published by Abdo Publishing, a division of ABDO, PO Box 398166, Minneapolis, Minnesota 55439.

Printed in the United States of America, North Mankato, Minnesota.
092019
012020

THIS BOOK CONTAINS
RECYCLED MATERIALS

Cover Photos: AP Images, letter; Eric Risberg/AP Images, sketch
Interior Photos: Bettmann/Getty Images, 5, 6, 15, 28, 44, 60–61, 67, 74, 87; Robert Clay/Alamy, 12; This Old Postcard/Alamy, 16–17; Justin Sullivan/Getty Images News/Getty Images, 23; AP Images, 25, 36, 52; Allen J. Schaben/Los Angeles Times/Getty Images, 35; Martin Klimek/Contour/Getty Images, 39; SJV/AP Images, 47, 78–79; Eric Risberg/AP Images, 48, 56–57; Rainer Lesniewski/iStockphoto, 59, 83; Susan Ehmer/San Francisco Chronicle/AP Images, 62; iStockphoto, 69; Craig Melville/Shutterstock Images, 77; Red Line Editorial, 86–87; Stephanie Strasburg/Pittsburgh Post-Gazette/AP Images, 91; TEK Image/Science Source, 97

Editor: Charly Haley
Series Designer: Melissa Martin

LIBRARY OF CONGRESS CONTROL NUMBER: 2019941970

PUBLISHER'S CATALOGING-IN-PUBLICATION DATA

Names: Mooney, Carla, author.
Title: The Zodiac Killer / by Carla Mooney
Description: Minneapolis, Minnesota: Abdo Publishing, 2020 | Series: American crime stories | Includes online resources and index.
Identifiers: ISBN 9781532190155 (lib. bdg) | ISBN 9781532176005 (ebook)
Subjects: LCSH: Serial killers--Juvenile literature. | Killing (Murder)--Juvenile literature. | Cold cases (Criminal investigation)--Juvenile literature. | Serial murder investigation--Juvenile literature. | Zodiac--Juvenile literature.
Classification: DDC 364.152--dc23

CONTENTS

CHAPTER ONE

ATTACK AT LOVERS' LANE

It was December 20, 1968—the last day of classes before winter break at Vallejo High School in Vallejo, California. Seventeen-year-old David Faraday, a good student and varsity athlete, was looking forward to his plans that Friday evening. He was going on a date with Betty Lou Jensen, a pretty 16-year-old from Hogan High School.

Friday Night Date

At 7:30 p.m., David left his home. He had dressed carefully for the date, wearing a light blue long-sleeve shirt and brown corduroy pants. David drove to Betty Lou's house in his mother's 1961 four-door station wagon. He arrived at about eight o'clock, parked the car, and walked to the door.

David Faraday

Like David, Betty Lou was a popular and hardworking student. For the date, she dressed in a purple minidress with white cuffs and a white collar. She wore a colored ribbon in her long brown hair and black T-strap shoes.

At the door, David helped Betty Lou put on her white fur coat. She told her parents that she and David were going to a Christmas carol concert at Hogan High, a few blocks from her house. Then the pair planned to go to a party after the concert. Betty Lou kissed her father goodbye and promised to be home by eleven o'clock.

Betty Lou Jensen, in a family photo

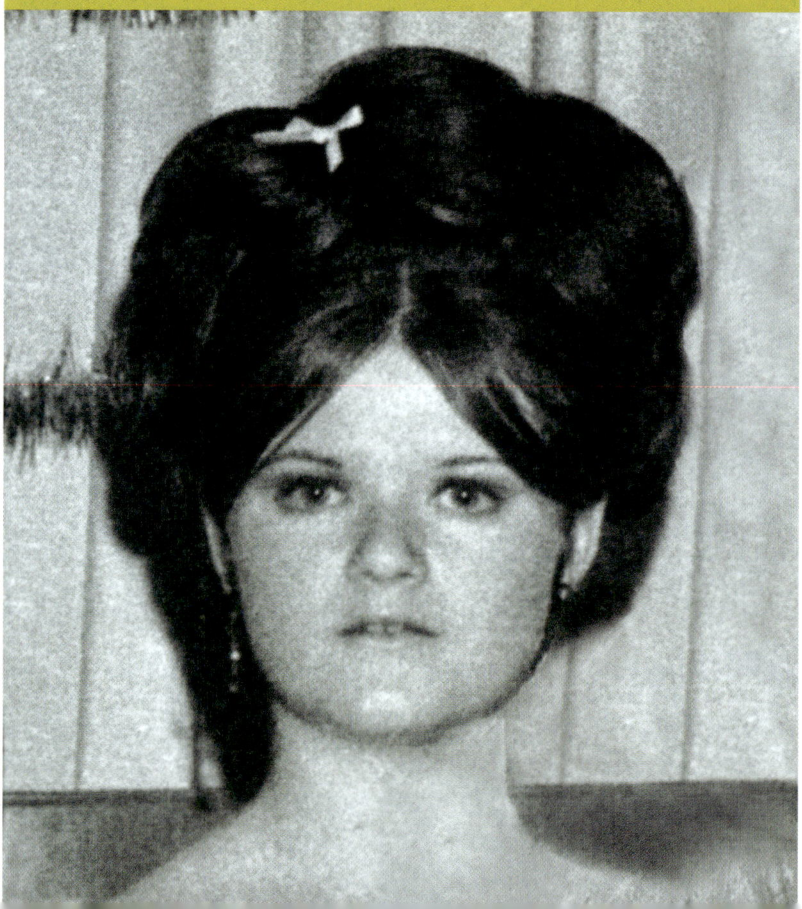

Last Seen Alive

At some point during their date, David and Betty Lou drove to Lake Herman Road, a few miles outside Vallejo's city limits. The remote area was a well-known lovers' lane, a popular spot for young romantic couples. David parked the station wagon in a clearing just off of the main road. He put Betty Lou's coat and purse, along with his sport coat, in the back seat.

Around eleven o'clock, Peggie and Homer Your drove to Lake Herman Road. Homer Your's company was installing sewer and water pipes in the area, and he wanted to check on the construction. The Yours passed the parked station wagon, and Peggie Your spotted David sitting in the driver's seat while Betty Lou leaned against his shoulder. After checking the construction site, the Yours turned around on Lake Herman Road a few minutes later. As they drove past the station wagon on their way out, the teens were still cuddling in the same position. It was the last time David and Betty Lou were seen together alive.

What Happened to David and Betty Lou?

Based on forensic evidence, investigators have put together a timeline for what they believe happened that night on Lake Herman Road. As the teens sat in the station wagon, a car approached. Unlike other cars, this one did not pass the station wagon. Instead, the driver drove off the remote road and stopped his car about ten feet (3 m) away from the station wagon.[1] The two cars sat side by side. Then the mysterious driver stepped out of his car and approached the station wagon, possibly ordering the young couple out of their car. As the man came closer, he pulled out a gun and shot out the station wagon's rear passenger window. Then he shot the left rear tire.

The couple must have been terrified and confused as they scrambled to get out of the car on the passenger side. Betty Lou jumped out first. As David tried to escape the car, the man reached through the open left window and pointed the barrel of his gun close to David's head, behind his left ear. He pulled the trigger, firing the bullet into David's head. The gun was so close that it left behind powder burns on the boy's ear.

Meanwhile, Betty Lou ran to escape. The

WHAT IS FORENSICS?

Every time a crime is committed, a criminal leaves evidence at the scene. Forensics is the science of finding that evidence and analyzing it for clues. Evidence may be a bloody handprint or a footprint on a dirt trail. A criminal might leave a strand of hair, a drop of sweat, or spent bullets from a fired gun. Each piece of evidence is a clue that provides information about what happened at the scene. Using scientific tools and principles, forensic scientists make careful observations and analyze evidence found at the crime scene. They present evidence in court with regard to the circumstances of a crime.

A CHANCE ENCOUNTER

Lorraine Osuna DeGroat believes she had a chance encounter with the man who murdered her friend Betty Lou Jensen. One night, a few months after Betty Lou's death, DeGroat and a few friends decided to visit the Lake Herman Road murder site. As they approached the isolated spot, they saw a man waving his arms in the middle of the road. The teens slowed their car as the man approached them. He said he needed help finding his girlfriend, who was lost on the lake. The man appeared to be in his mid-30s to early 40s, with short hair and horn-rimmed glasses. The teens felt uneasy, as the man seemed too calm and was completely dry, indicating that he probably hadn't been looking for someone in the lake. Instead of stopping, the teens raced away and drove straight to the Benicia Police Department. Police investigated their report but found no one at the scene and no missing persons reported.

gunman followed her and fired repeatedly. He shot Betty Lou five times in her back. She fell to the ground about 28 feet (8.5 m) from the station wagon.[2] The man walked to his car and drove away.

A Gruesome Discovery

At 11:10 p.m., Stella Borges, who lived on a ranch on Lake Herman Road, got into her car to pick up her son in Benicia. About five minutes later, Borges came upon the site where the teens had been gunned down. She saw the two victims in the glow of her headlights. Frightened, she sped down the road until she found a Benicia police car. She flashed her headlights and honked her car horn to get the police officers' attention. Borges told Captain Daniel Pitta and Officer William Warner what she had seen.

Classmates of David Faraday and Betty Lou Jensen organized a reward fund to help catch the killer.

The officers raced to Lake Herman Road with their police lights flashing. When they arrived, they found David barely alive. They immediately called for an ambulance. They found Betty Lou's lifeless body and covered her with a wool blanket. Then they called for backup from the Solano County Sheriff's Office.

Detective Leslie Lundblad of the sheriff's office led the investigation. He made a sketch of the scene, working by flashlight and later by floodlights. Other investigators took photographs of the scene and dusted the station wagon for fingerprints. They searched the area for the gun and other pieces of evidence. They recovered shell casings that identified

A SUSPECT WITH AN ALIBI

As part of the murder investigation, police looked into the private lives of both victims. Betty Lou's family told the police about a boy who had been obsessed with her, harassing her at school and even threatening David. Betty Lou's family even suspected that the boy had been sneaking around their yard at night. Detective Lundblad investigated the potential suspect and found the boy had an alibi for the night of the killings. He had attended his sister's birthday party and then watched a television show until eleven o'clock with a police officer from Mare Island.

the ammunition the gunman had used as Winchester Western Super-X copper-coated bullets. Ballistic evidence suggested the killer had used a .22-caliber gun, possibly a J. C. Higgins Model 80 semiautomatic pistol. The gun itself was not found. Because the ground was frozen, there were no tire tracks. Police found just a few faint footprints.

Lundblad ordered two of his officers to get a statement from David. When the officers arrived at the hospital, they learned David had died in the ambulance. There were no witnesses who could tell police what exactly had happened to these two teens on that dark December night.

MATCHING BULLETS TO A GUN

Police recovered seven bullets from the victims and the car. Four of the bullets were in good condition, while the other three were damaged. When a gun fires a bullet, it leaves identifying markings on the bullet. Similar to fingerprints, the markings made by an individual gun are unique. Therefore, forensic specialists can use the markings to match a bullet to the gun that fired it. They do this by firing the gun and comparing the markings on the test bullet to the markings on the bullet found at the crime scene. But at the Lake Herman crime scene, the police did not find a gun. They had no gun to test to match the bullets recovered at the scene.

A Puzzling Case

In their search for the violent attacker, police questioned David's and Betty Lou's families and friends. They reconstructed the teens' last day, almost minute

Graffiti along Lake Herman Road, where David and Betty Lou were killed, shows the symbol of the Zodiac killer.

QUESTIONING CLASSMATES

Police questioned Betty Lou's and David's friends and classmates to see if they had any information that could help find the killer. Sharon Henslin Stutsman was one of Betty Lou's best friends and shared a locker with her at Hogan High School. Years later, she spoke about being questioned by police, saying it was a terrifying experience. According to Stutsman, the police first believed the murders were connected to drugs. They asked Stutsman and other teens about who at school did drugs and came up with a theory that Betty Lou and David had been at a drug party on Lake Herman Road the night they were killed. Stutsman insisted this was not possible because Betty Lou and David were not drug users.

by minute. They dug deep into the private lives of the victims. Who could have wanted them dead? The police followed up on many leads and tips from the public. None were successful. Despite their efforts, the police had no suspects or motives for the puzzling murders. And they didn't realize these murders would be the first in a series of mysterious killings by a man known only as the Zodiac. The murders remain unsolved.

CHAPTER TWO

FOURTH OF JULY MURDER

Nearly six months later, on July 4, 1969, 22-year-old Darlene Ferrin and her 15-year-old sister, Christina, stopped at Caesar's Palace Italian Restaurant in Vallejo. Ferrin's husband, Dean, worked there as an assistant cook. Darlene Ferrin was a friendly and well-liked waitress at Terry's Restaurant, also in Vallejo. She knew many of her customers well and was known for being friendly to everyone she met. "Darlene was happy, laughing, joking, outgoing, not shy, talkative. . . . She didn't mind meeting new people, new friends," said Bobbie Ramos, who worked at Terry's with her.[1]

At Caesar's, Ferrin told her husband that she and Christina were on their way to Mare Island for a Fourth of July celebration and boat parade. Dean asked what time Ferrin planned to be home. He reminded her that he had invited some coworkers and friends over to the couple's house for a small party later

Darlene Ferrin

Ferrin lived and worked in Vallejo, California.

that evening, after he finished his shift at the restaurant. Ferrin replied that she would be home by ten o'clock and agreed to pick up some fireworks for the party.

Meeting Mike

When Darlene Ferrin arrived home, she greeted the two teenage babysitters who were watching her and Dean's daughter, Dena. She changed her clothes and was about to drive the babysitters home when the phone rang. Ferrin

answered it and spoke briefly. After she hung up, she asked if the two babysitters could stay a little longer. She told them she needed to go back out and buy fireworks for the party. The sitters agreed, and Ferrin left.

Instead of getting fireworks, Ferrin drove her Chevy Corvair to the house of her friend, 19-year-old Mike Mageau. She arrived at about 11:30 p.m. Mageau rushed outside and got into the Corvair, leaving the lights and television on and the door open to his house.

A Car Follows

As they drove away, Mageau noticed a light-colored car following them. Ferrin made several turns to lose the car, but it stayed with them. Eventually, Ferrin pulled into the parking lot of the Blue Rock Springs golf course, about four miles (6 km) from downtown Vallejo. The parking lot was only a few miles from the place where Betty Lou Jensen and David Faraday were killed. As she drove through the lot, Ferrin stalled the car's engine.

As Ferrin and Mageau sat in the Corvair, the other car entered the lot, turned off its lights, and parked about eight feet (2.4 m) from them.[2] As Ferrin and Mageau nervously waited to see what would happen, the car drove off. They breathed a sigh of relief and sat talking and listening to music.

THE PAINTING PARTY STALKER

In May 1969, Darlene and Dean Ferrin bought a small house in Vallejo. They held a painting party with family and friends to help them clean up the house. At the party, Darlene Ferrin's sister Linda Del Buono remembers seeing a stocky man who seemed out of place. Ferrin was surprised the man had come and seemed frightened of him. She begged Del Buono to stay away from the man. According to Del Buono, the man was about five feet, eight inches tall (1.72 m) and overweight. He had curly hair and dark-rimmed glasses. Ferrin's other sister, Pam Huckaby, who was also at the painting party, said she also noticed the strange man. When someone else asked Ferrin about him, Huckaby said, Ferrin told them not to worry. The police did not investigate this lead because Ferrin's sisters did not come forward with this information about an alleged stalker until many years after Ferrin died.

About five minutes later, the car returned. This time, it pulled up behind them, blocking the Corvair. Suddenly, a bright light shined from the other car.

The initial Vallejo Police Department police report listed "Jealousy-Revenge" as the apparent motive for the attack on Ferrin and Mageau.[3]

The car's driver opened his door and walked toward the couple, blazing the bright light into their faces. Thinking it might be a police officer, Mageau reached for his wallet and told Ferrin to get her identification out of her purse.

Shot without Warning

The driver strode to the open passenger window where Mageau sat. Before Mageau could show his ID, the man pulled out a gun and fired at him and Ferrin. He shot several times at the couple. Several bullets passed through Mageau's body and hit Ferrin. She slumped forward over the steering wheel. Without saying a word, the shooter walked back to his car.

In great pain, Mageau cried out. The shooter stopped and looked back at him. For the first time, Mageau got a glimpse of the shooter's face. The man looked to be between 26 and 30 years old and had a large face. He had short, curly brown hair in a military-style crew cut. About five feet, eight inches tall (1.72 m), he was stocky and appeared to weigh nearly 200 pounds (91 kg).

The shooter walked back to the Corvair. He leaned through the open window and shot twice more at Mageau and Ferrin. Then he got into his car and quickly drove away. Badly wounded, Mageau opened the passenger door and fell from the car onto the parking lot. He heard Ferrin moan from the front seat.

Calls for Help

A short time later, three teens driving through the area spotted Mageau on the ground. Alive but severely injured, Mageau told the teens that he had been shot and needed help. The teens called the police. When officers arrived, they found Mageau lying at the rear of the Corvair, bleeding badly from gunshots to his face, neck, chest, shoulders, and left leg. Ferrin was slumped over the steering wheel. Detective John Lynch and Sergeant Ed Rust from the Vallejo Police Department recognized her

FERRIN'S BOYFRIENDS

Some people have theorized that Ferrin and Mageau were attacked by a jilted lover. Although she was married, Ferrin was known to date several men in town, including at least one policeman. She often went out and did not come home until the early hours of the morning. Several people reported seeing Ferrin in different places with other men. Her husband, Dean, insisted that she was young and enjoying herself, and he said she was not doing anything wrong. A few of Ferrin's friends remembered one man named Paul who kept trying to date Ferrin and got upset when she turned him down. Investigators tracked him down and questioned him, but they eventually cleared him as a suspect because he had an alibi for the night of the attack.

THE EX-HUSBAND

For a short time, police considered Ferrin's ex-husband, Jim Phillips (also known as Jim Crabree), as a potential suspect. Ferrin had married Phillips in January 1966 in Reno, Nevada. She filed for divorce from him in 1967. In her divorce filing, she claimed that Phillips had treated her with extreme mental cruelty. She also said that he hit her when he was angry. After her murder, the police tracked down Phillips in Santa Cruz, California, and questioned him for any information he might have about Ferrin and her murder. They quickly ruled him out as a suspect.

immediately. Many police officers stopped at Terry's, where she worked. Lynch called for an ambulance.

Despite being badly injured, Mageau tried to tell Lynch what had happened. When he tried to speak, blood gushed from his mouth. With great difficulty, he told Lynch, "A white man drove up in a car, got out, walked up to the car, shined a flashlight inside, started shooting," he said.[4] He also gave a brief description—a younger man, heavyset, driving a light tan car. He told Lynch that the man never said a word throughout the attack.

In the car, Ferrin was still alive and softly moaning. She tried to tell Lynch something. He leaned close to her but was unable to make out what she was saying. When the ambulance arrived, Officer Richard Hoffman from the Vallejo Police Department went with the victims to the hospital, just in case Ferrin recovered enough to talk. She never did. Ferrin died on the way to the hospital. She was declared dead at 12:38 a.m. At the hospital, Mageau was rushed into surgery. He survived.

Looking for Evidence

Meanwhile, police combed the parking lot for evidence. They illuminated the area with floodlights to help them see. One officer made a detailed sketch of the entire crime scene. In their search, police found several shell casings and bullets, which appeared to be from either a 9 mm or .38 caliber gun. However, no gun was found. Because the killer fired between nine and 13 shots without reloading, the police believed the gun was most likely a Browning, which could hold 13 cartridges. No other semiautomatic gun at the time held more than seven or eight bullets.

POTENTIAL IDENTIFICATION

In 1991, George Bawart of the Vallejo Police Department showed survivor Mike Mageau a photo lineup of suspects. Mageau identified suspect Arthur Leigh Allen as the man who shot him and killed Darlene Ferrin. When Bawart asked Mageau why he hadn't identified Allen in the 20-plus years since the shooting, Mageau explained that he had never been shown any photos of potential suspects. Police had only asked him if he recognized any names. Despite presenting Mageau the photo lineup in 1991, police ended up deciding that Mageau's answer was not accurate and could not be relied upon in the investigation.

A Call to Police

At 12:40 a.m., exactly two minutes after Ferrin was declared dead, a man

The first known phone call from the Zodiac killer was to the Vallejo Police Department shortly after the attack on Ferrin and Mageau.

called the Vallejo Police Department. Switchboard operator Nancy Slover answered the call. The man did not identify himself. In a calm yet forceful voice, he said, "I want to report a double murder. If you will go one mile east on Columbus Parkway to the public park, you will find kids in a brown car."[5] When Slover tried to interrupt him to get more information, the caller simply talked over her. Slover reported that he did not have an accent and sounded mature. "They were shot with a 9-millimeter Luger. I also killed those kids last year. Goodbye," the caller said.[6] Then he hung up. With the help of the telephone company, the police traced the call. It had been placed from a pay phone a few blocks from the Vallejo Police Department.

CHAPTER THREE

MYSTERIOUS LETTERS FROM THE KILLER

On August 1, 1969, about a month after Darlene Ferrin was murdered, the editorial staff of the *San Francisco Chronicle* newspaper received a mysterious letter. It arrived in an envelope, with no return address, that had been postmarked in San Francisco. The sender had written, "Please Rush to Editor!" on the envelope.[1] The handwritten letter itself contained a chilling message: "Dear Editor This is the murderer of the 2 teenagers last Christmass at Lake Herman & the girl on the 4th of July near the golf course in Vallejo."[2]

Was the letter a prank? To prove it was not, the sender then listed several facts about the murders and crime scenes that only the police and the killer were likely to know. The sender wrote the brand of ammunition used in both the Christmas and

The Zodiac killer sent several cryptic handwritten letters in 1969 and the early 1970s.

This is the Zodiac speaking

I though you would need a good laugh before you hear the bad news you won't get the news for a while yet.

PS could you print this new cipher on your front page? I get awfully lonely when I am ignored, so lonely I could do my Thing!!!!!!

and i can't do a thing with it!

Des July Aug Sept Oct = 7

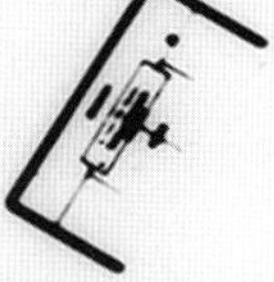

Fourth of July murders. He described how many shots were fired, what the victims were wearing, and how they were left at the scene. Editors at two other area newspapers, the *San Francisco Examiner* and the *Vallejo Times-Herald*, received similar versions of the menacing letter. Each one was signed with the same symbol—a circle with a cross drawn through it. The mysterious symbol would become the killer's signature.

A Coded Message

Each letter also contained one-third of a cryptogram. A cryptogram is a type of coded message. Each third of the cryptogram had eight lines with 17 symbols each. The symbols included Greek letters, Morse code, weather symbols, alphabet characters, and astrological symbols. The sender teased that if someone could solve the cryptogram, his identity would be revealed.

The letters ordered each newspaper to print the cryptogram on their front pages. If the newspapers did not print the coded messages, the letter writer threatened to go on a killing rampage that weekend, targeting random victims.

The Zodiac never explained why he chose a cross inside a circle as his symbol.

After making photocopies of the letters and cryptograms, the newspapers sent the originals to Detective Lynch

WHAT IS CRYPTOGRAPHY?

The Zodiac killer used knowledge of cryptography to send coded messages to the press and police. Cryptography is the practice and study of hiding information. When a message is sent using cryptography, it is changed or encrypted before being sent. The method of changing the text is called a cipher. Using a cipher to change the text makes the message hard to read. A cipher rearranges letters or uses substitute symbols to represent letters and disguise the message. The person receiving the message must first decrypt it or change it back in order to read it.

at the Vallejo Police Department. They also called in expert codebreakers to help solve the cipher. The Vallejo police sent copies of the code to Naval Intelligence at the Mare Island Naval Shipyard. Codebreaking experts at the National Security Agency (NSA), the Federal Bureau of Investigation (FBI), and the Central Intelligence Agency (CIA) were also asked to help solve the cryptogram. Despite their efforts, the cryptogram remained unsolved.

The *Times-Herald* and the *Chronicle* each printed their respective thirds of the coded message in their next edition. The *San Francisco Examiner* waited to run its portion of the coded message until Sunday, August 3. It also printed the portion of the coded message sent to the other two newspapers. For the first time, the entire coded message appeared publicly in one place.

Donald Harden, a school teacher, and his wife, Bettye, worked to decipher the Zodiac killer's first cryptogram. After that, the Hardens were not involved with investigating the Zodiac any further.

Breaking the Code

That Sunday morning, Donald Harden opened his newspaper. Harden was a 41-year-old history and economics teacher at North Salinas High School, about 100 miles (160 km) south of San Francisco. Ever since he was young, Harden had been interested in codebreaking. He decided to try his hand at figuring out the cipher used to create the cryptogram. Harden grabbed one of his old codebreaking books and cleared a workspace at the dining room table.

After studying the cryptogram for some time, Harden decided that it had been created with a substitution cipher. In this type of cipher, every letter of the alphabet is replaced by a letter, figure, or symbol. Harden worked, using neat capital letters, and checked the frequency of the symbols in the coded message. He knew that the letter E is the most common letter in English, followed by T, A, O, N, I, R, and S. He also knew that the most common letters that appear twice in a row in English are L, E, and S. Therefore, if the message had two identical symbols next to each other, it was probably one of those letters. Harden also looked for common letter combinations—TH, HE, and AN.

The Zodiac wrote in a small, cramped style that trailed downward toward the right. He often used a blue felt-tip pen.

However, as Harden worked, he began to think that the cipher contained so many symbols it was unlikely the person who made it had used a one-for-one substitution. For hours, Harden studied the cryptogram and searched for repeating patterns of symbols. Harden's wife, Bettye June Harden, then sat down and began working on the cipher with him. They worked for the rest of the day and into the night. Eventually, they went to bed with the cipher still unsolved.

The next morning, Harden was ready to give up on figuring out the cipher. His wife, however, wanted to keep working on it. Eventually, he joined her back at the dining room table. Bettye Harden believed that the killer was extremely self-centered. As a result, she guessed that any message he or she sent would start with the word *I*. She also thought the killer would use the word *killing* in the message. Following this hunch, the Hardens had a breakthrough. The message had places where two identical symbols were repeated. Since one of the most common double letters in English is L, they began looking for four symbol patterns that could represent the word *kill*.

HOW TO SOLVE A BASIC SUBSTITUTION CIPHER

A substitution cipher is one that substitutes symbols or other letters for the letters in a message. To solve a basic substitution cipher, codebreakers use several steps:

- Scan the cipher and look for single-letter words. They are probably a or I.
- Count how many times each symbol appears in the coded message. The most frequent symbol is probably an E. Other possible common letters are T, A, or O.
- Look for apostrophes. The symbols following an apostrophe are probably D, LL, M, RE, S, or T.
- Look for repeating symbols. They may be common two- and three-letter combinations such as TH, SH, RE, CH, TR, ING, ION, and ENT.
- Try to guess on deciphering two-, three-, and four-letter words. The most common two-letter words in English are of, to, in, is, and it.
- Look for double symbols, which are most likely LL, EE, SS, OO, and TT.

Slowly, the Hardens began to unravel the cipher and decode the message. Still, the work was not easy. In several places, the killer had misspelled words and did not use punctuation. Also, the killer had used several tricks to make the cipher more difficult to break. Because E is the most common letter in English, the killer used the symbol of a backward Q several times to trick them into thinking it represented E. For the real letter E in the message, however, the killer used seven different symbols. The killer also used two different symbols to stand for A and S.

After 20 hours, the Hardens finally cracked the code. The first part of the message read:

I LIKE KILLING PEOPLE

BECAUSE IT IS SO MUCH

FUN IT IS MORE FUN THAN

KILLING WILD GAME IN

THE FORREST BECAUSE

MAN IS THE MOST DANGEROUE

ANAMAL OF ALL TO KILL[3]

The message went on to state that the killer believed all of his victims would become his slaves in the afterlife. The Hardens could not find anything in the cryptogram that revealed the killer's identity. However, at the end of the

THE KILLER'S NAME

On August 12, the Hardens' solution to the cipher was published in the paper. Amateur codebreakers wondered what the letters at the end of the deciphered message could be. Many theorized that it might be an anagram for the killer's name. An anagram is a word or phrase that is formed by rearranging the letters of another word or phrase. They attempted to come up with names that worked with these letters. However, no real leads to the killer's identity came from these attempts.

message, there was a series of letters that had little meaning: "EBEORIETEMETHHPITI."[4] Perhaps that could be the clue to the killer's identity?

Donald Harden called the *Chronicle* and reported that he had solved the cipher. However, the paper had received hundreds of calls from people claiming to have information about the printed cryptogram. The editor told Harden to mail his solution to the paper, which would pass it along to police.

After police received the Hardens' solution, Naval Intelligence experts double-checked their work. These experts declared that the couple had been able to successfully decipher the message that had stumped code experts at the CIA, FBI, and NSA. Yet, despite the success with the cryptogram, the police were no closer to figuring out the identity of the killer.

The Zodiac

Meanwhile, Vallejo Police Chief Jack Stiltz was not convinced that the letter had been written by the killer. While Stiltz admitted that the letter had some details of the murders that were not general public knowledge, he insisted it was information anyone who had talked to someone at the crime scene could know. Stiltz publicly asked the sender to write another letter and include more facts to prove he or she was the killer.

On August 4, the *Examiner* received a three-page letter. With this letter, for the first time, the killer gave himself a name. He called himself the Zodiac. The letter contained many details about the killings. The letter began, "This is the Zodiac speaking. In answer to your asking for more details about the good times I have had in Vallejo, I shall be very happy to supply even more material. By the way, are the police haveing a good time with the code?"[5]

HOW DID THE ZODIAC GET HIS NAME?

In his August 4 letter to the *Examiner*, the killer gave himself a name: Zodiac. Where did that name come from? Although no one knows for sure, there are several theories. One theory is that the killer took the name Zodiac from a watch. Founded in 1882, the Zodiac watch brand has made stylish watches for over a century. The Zodiac brand also had a symbol—a circle with a cross drawn through it. Although the Zodiac killer has never been identified, one of the suspects, Arthur Leigh Allen, owned a Zodiac Sea Wolf watch.

CHAPTER FOUR

A HOODED ATTACKER AT THE LAKE

After the August 4 letter, the Zodiac went quiet for a few weeks. Police worked tirelessly, following lead after lead to uncover the killer's identity. But their efforts were unsuccessful. Then on September 27, 1969, the Zodiac struck again.

A Beautiful Day at the Lake

Cecelia Ann Shepard, a 22-year-old student at Pacific Union College in Angwin, California, had decided to transfer to the University of California in Riverside to study music. On September 27, she planned to pack up her belongings at Pacific Union College so they could be shipped to her new school. Fellow student Bryan Hartnell, her good friend, offered to

The Zodiac's third attack happened at Lake Berryessa, on the north edge of the San Francisco Bay Area.

Cecelia Ann Shepard, *left*, and Bryan Hartnell

help her pack. The pair met early in the morning at the school, attended church, and then packed Shepard's things into boxes.

After they finished packing, the pair walked to the college cafeteria for lunch. Hartnell asked Shepard if she had any plans for the afternoon. They decided to drive to Lake Berryessa together. At about four o'clock, Hartnell parked his white Volkswagen Karmann Ghia on the edge of the road near the lake. The area was deserted, with no other cars. Hartnell and Shepard walked about one-quarter mile (0.4 km) until they found a good spot for a picnic on the lake's shoreline. They spread a blanket on the ground. As the sun flashed off the lake water, the pair relaxed and embraced. From their blanket, they could see Goat Island and an occasional boat.

A Strange Man Lurking

After some time, Shepard noticed a man lurking nearby. He appeared stocky, with dark brown hair. Then he disappeared into a grove of trees about 250 yards (230 m) away.[1] Moments later, the man emerged from the grove of trees and slowly moved toward the couple. Shepard warned Hartnell that they were not alone. Unconcerned, Hartnell did not move from the blanket. Shepard grew uneasy at the man's strange behavior. He seemed to be watching them.

BEING FOLLOWED AT LAKE BERRYESSA

A few hours before Hartnell and Shepard arrived at Lake Berryessa, three young women were also on their way to the lake. As they parked their car near a fast-food restaurant, another car driven by a man pulled up next to them and backed up so that his car's rear bumper was even with their car. The man sat in his car looking down as if he were reading. The women estimated the man to be about 25 to 35 years old, with dark hair parted on the side. They thought he was about six feet (1.8 m) tall and weighed more than 200 pounds (90 kg). The women drove off to the lake. About an hour later, as they sunbathed on the shoreline, they spotted the same man watching them. After about 20 minutes, he drove away. Some people believe this man may have been the Zodiac killer.

While Shepard looked away for a moment, the man disappeared again behind a nearby oak tree. When he emerged from behind the tree, the man wore a black hood over his head and face, with holes cut into the cloth for his eyes and mouth. The man covered the hood's eye slits with clip-on sunglasses. The hood had front and back panels that covered his chest and back. The front panel was decorated with a cross placed over a circle. The man also wore a sheath that held a long knife. Several lengths of white plastic clothesline hung from under the man's jacket. The man pointed a semiautomatic pistol at Shepard and Hartnell.

Descriptions of the Zodiac killer's clothing led police to believe he was a military man. The hood he wore at Lake Berryessa was well-sewn, a skill required in the US Navy.

A Vicious Attack

Shepard grabbed Hartnell's arm as the man walked straight toward them. When he reached the blanket, the man spoke. "I want your money and your car keys," he said.[2] Hartnell reached into his pockets and handed over everything he had, including the keys to his car. The masked man tossed the keys on the blanket and placed the gun in a holster on his right side. He told the couple that he had escaped from a prison in Montana and had killed a prison guard. He warned them that he had nothing to lose.

Although he hoped the man would take the keys and money and leave, Hartnell's hopes sank when the man took out a clothesline. He ordered Hartnell to lie facedown on the ground. Hartnell thought about trying to wrestle the gun away from the man, but he feared Shepard would get hurt in the struggle. Instead, Hartnell decided to cooperate with the masked man.

Based on witness descriptions, journalist and author Robert Graysmith made these sketches of the man who attacked Shepard and Hartnell.

The man ordered Shepard to bind Hartnell with the clothesline. She wound the line around his hands and feet using a few loose knots. When she finished, the man tied her up. He discovered the loose knots on Hartnell and retied them extremely tight.

Once bound, Hartnell and Shepard were helpless. The man talked to them quietly for a few minutes. He showed Hartnell that the gun was loaded. Then he announced in a husky voice, "I'm going to have to stab you people."[3]

For the first time, Hartnell feared for his life. Not wanting Shepard to be hurt, he begged the man to stab him first. The man pulled the knife from its sheath and raised it high over Hartnell's head. He stabbed Hartnell in his back repeatedly. As blood spurted from his wounds, Hartnell stiffened and collapsed from the pain. The man then turned to Shepard. He stabbed her many times in her

ANOTHER ENCOUNTER

Another visitor at the lake may have had a chance encounter with the Zodiac killer that day. A dentist and his young son parked their car and walked down to the lake's beach. They noticed a man watching them. The heavyset man was about five feet, ten inches (1.78 m) tall and wearing dark pants and a dark long-sleeve shirt. The man realized that the dentist and his son had seen him. He also probably noticed that the dentist's son carried a .22 rifle. He turned quickly and walked in the opposite direction. Later, tire tracks showed that the man's car had been parked directly behind the dentist's car.

back. When she rolled over to escape, the man stabbed her chest, groin, and abdomen as she begged him to stop. Hartnell knew that there was nothing he could do to save Shepard and pretended to be dead. At last, the man stood up, slowly walked away, and disappeared.

Help Arrives

Hartnell and Shepard most likely passed out for a little bit. When they regained consciousness, they tried to yell for help. Hartnell twisted himself so that he could use his teeth to slowly loosen the clothesline tied around Shepard's wrists. When she was free, Shepard untied Hartnell's hands. Hartnell planned to crawl for help, but he had lost so much blood he was too weak to move.

On the lake, a fisherman and his son heard moans coming from the shore and rowed closer to see what it was. Scared by the terrible sight, they rowed to get help. At a nearby resort, they alerted park rangers.

Meanwhile, Hartnell's heart sank as the fisherman rowed away. Believing no one was coming to help, he started crawling toward the road. He made it about 300 yards (270 m) when Park Ranger Dennis Land found him lying alongside the dirt road.[4] Hartnell told Land that Shepard was still on the shore. Land hurried to help her.

Ranger Sergeant William White and the owners of the resort arrived by boat. They wrapped Hartnell and Shepard in blankets as they waited for an ambulance to arrive from the closest hospital, nearly an hour away. While they waited, the badly injured couple tried to tell rangers as many details as they could about the attack. However, they were both in great pain and drifted in and out of consciousness. When the ambulance arrived, paramedics rushed the two victims to the hospital. Two days later, Shepard died from her injuries. Hartnell survived.

After giving several interviews in the first years after the Lake Berryessa attack, Hartnell no longer talks to the news media about it.

A Call to the Sheriff

At 7:40 p.m., a little more than an hour after the stabbings, the phone rang at the Napa County Sheriff's Office. When the operator answered the phone, the caller told her that he wanted to report a double murder at Lake Berryessa. The caller told the operator where to find the victims and even described the victims' car. Then he told the operator that he was the one who had done it. The caller put the telephone receiver down, but he did not hang up.

DUSTING AND LIFTING A PRINT

When examining a crime scene, police often look for fingerprints that they can use to link a suspect to the crime. To lift the palm print on the pay phone receiver outside the sheriff's office, the print had to first be dried with artificial light. Once the print was dry, crime scene investigators dusted the surface of the phone receiver. A print must be dry before it is dusted so the powder will stick to the acids left by the person's hand, instead of sticking to any moisture on the surface. After dusting the print, the investigators photographed it and lifted it with clear adhesive tape. The lifted print was then placed on a special card that is used to preserve and document the print so it could be compared to prints from possible suspects.

The police quickly traced the call to a car wash pay phone that was only four and a half blocks from the sheriff's office. This time, the Zodiac left a clue behind. Police were able to lift a latent palm print from the telephone receiver. A latent print is a print left on a surface by deposits of oils and sweat from a person's fingers or palm.

Another Message from the Zodiac

Detective Sergeant Kenneth Narlow of the Napa County Sheriff's Office led the investigation at the lake. He ordered officers to look for anyone who may have seen something suspicious in the area. When he saw Hartnell's white Volkswagen, he noticed the killer had left a message written in black felt-tip pen on the car's door. It read:

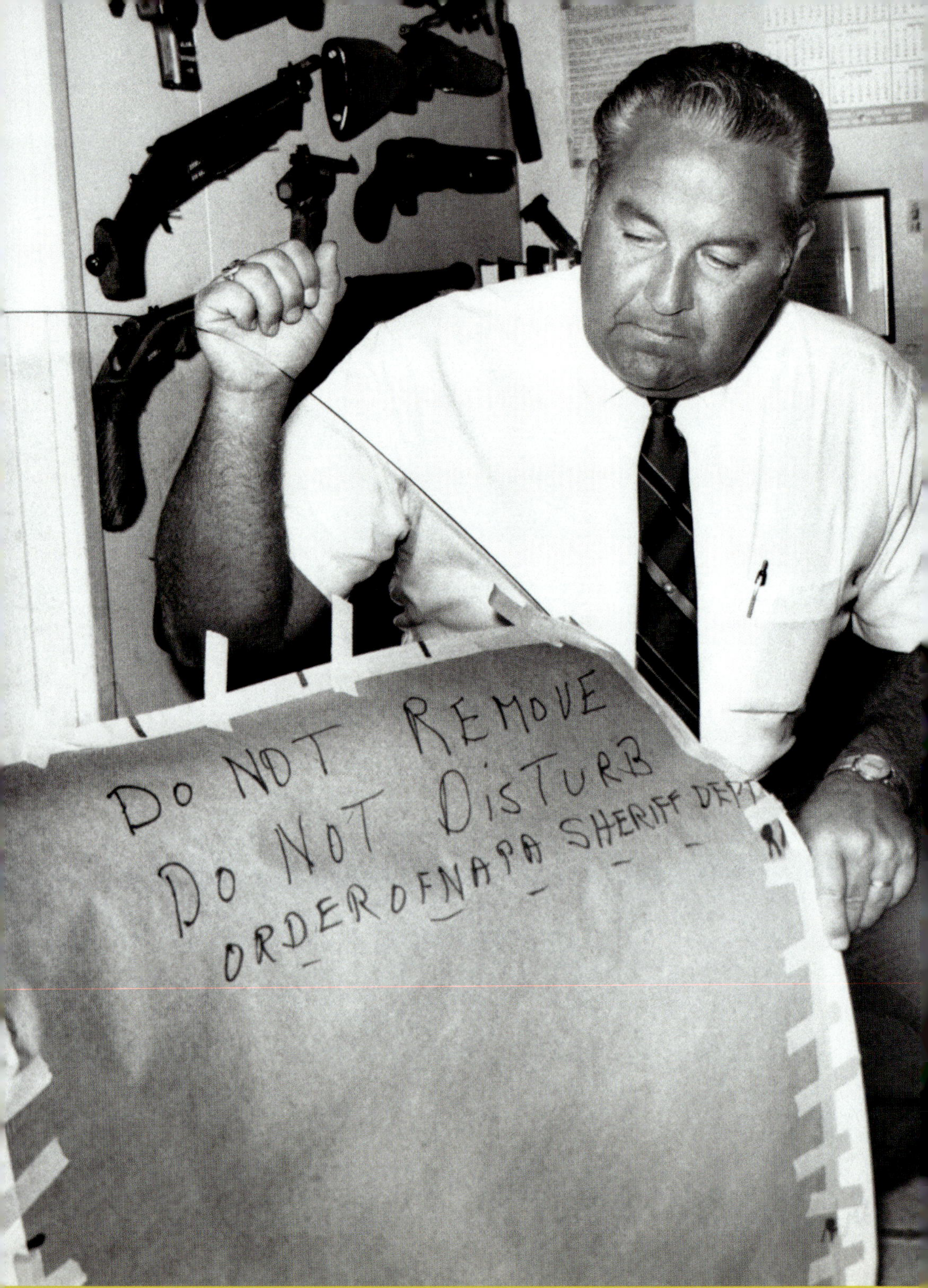

Sheriff's department investigators took Hartnell's car door as evidence.

Vallejo

12-20-68

7-4-69

Sept 27-69-6:30

by knife[5]

Narlow realized immediately what the message meant. The first dates matched those of the two previous attacks linked to the Zodiac killer. The third date referred to the attack on Shepard and Hartnell. According to the message, the Zodiac was responsible for all of the attacks. In case there was any doubt, the killer had also drawn the symbol of the Zodiac—a circle with a cross—on the car door.

WHAT IS A LATENT PRINT?

Everyone's hands and fingers produce oils and sweat. When a person touches a surface, part of these oils and sweat transfer to the surface. A latent fingerprint or palm print is a print left on a surface by these deposits of oils and sweat. Latent prints are not usually able to be seen by the naked eye. Crime scene investigators can find latent prints using special techniques such as dusting a surface with a fine powder that sticks to the oils and sweat left on the surface. The print's pattern revealed by the powder can be lifted with clear adhesive tape and placed on a latent print card. Investigators can then use these cards to compare the prints to known suspects.

CHAPTER FIVE

PRESIDIO HEIGHTS MURDER

The attack at Lake Berryessa provided police with more evidence than the Zodiac's earlier attacks. It gave investigators the palm print from the pay phone receiver that the Zodiac had used to call the Napa County Sheriff's Office. Investigators also had the message the Zodiac had written on Hartnell's car door. Officers also found the tire tracks left by the attacker's car. They made plaster casts called moulages of the tracks. From the tracks, investigators determined that the Zodiac's car had two different-size tires on the front, both of which were very worn. They estimated the width between the wheels to be about 57 inches (145 cm).

Officers from the San Francisco Police Department and the Napa County Sheriff's Office compare notes on the Zodiac case.

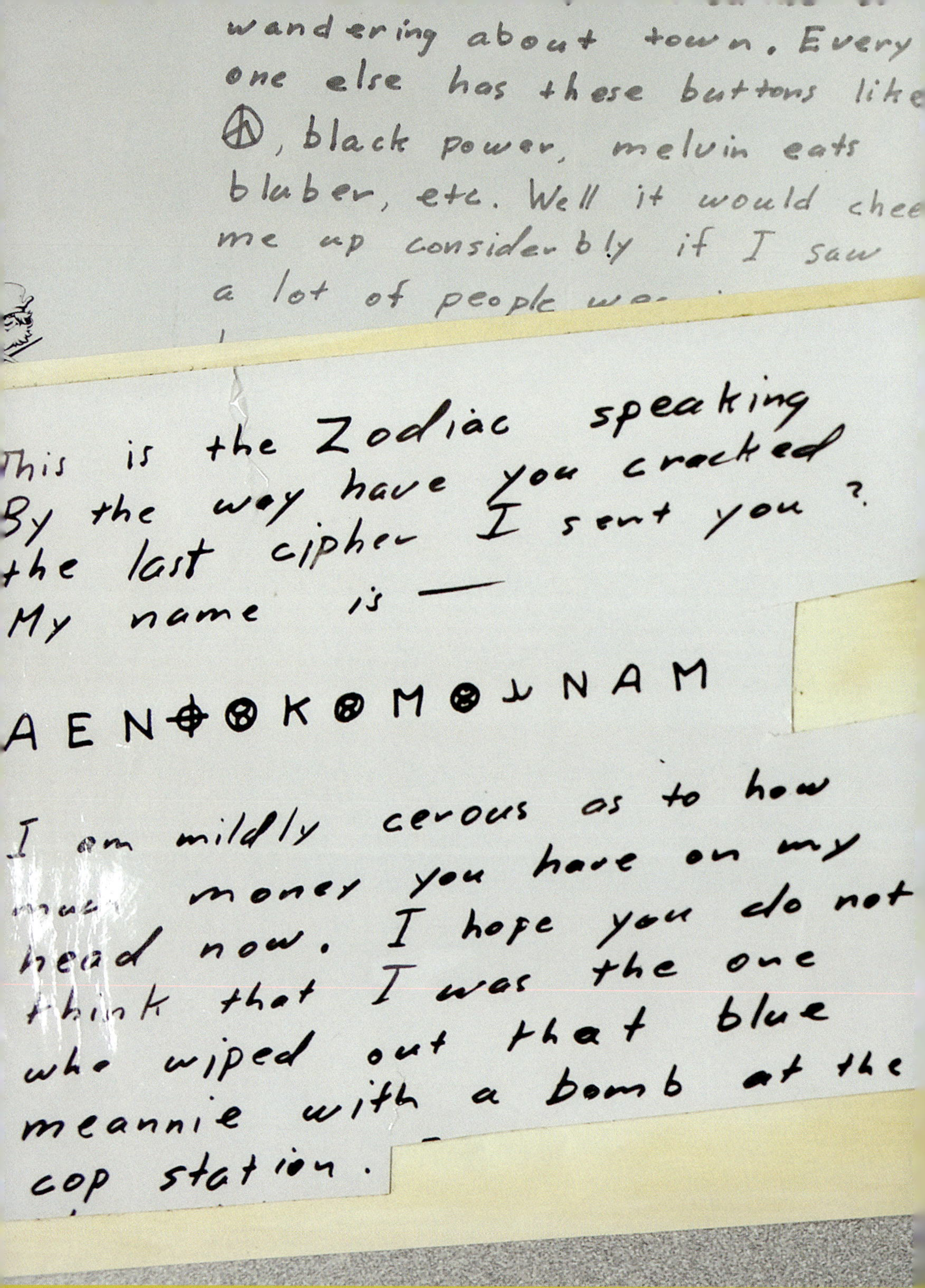

wandering about town. Every
one else has these buttons like
☮, black power, melvin eats
bluber, etc. Well it would chee
me up considerbly if I saw
a lot of people wea

This is the Zodiac speaking
By the way have you cracked
the last cipher I sent you?
My name is —

AEN⊕⊗K⊗M⊗⫝NAM

I am mildly cerous as to how
much money you have on my
head now. I hope you do not
think that I was the one
who wiped out that blue
meannie with a bomb at the
cop station.

Investigators examined the Zodiac's letters using handwriting analysis.

Gathering More Evidence

Crime scene investigators also found a footprint on the path leading to Hartnell's car. The same footprints led down to the crime scene and back up the hill to the road. Investigators made plaster casts of the footprints, which, once measured, turned out to be shoe size 10.5. Detective Narlow noticed that the footprints were very deep in the ground. He called for one of the heavier officers at the scene to walk on the ground next to the footprints. The officer weighed about 210 pounds (95 kg), and his steps did not sink as deeply into the trail as the Zodiac's had. As a result, investigators estimated that the attacker weighed about 220 pounds (100 kg).

Narlow knelt on the sandy rock and studied the footprints. Between the heel and the sole, he noticed a little circle with printing. Investigators used that marking to identify the boots that had made the prints, a type of military boot called Wing Walkers. This clue led investigators to believe the Zodiac was involved with the military in some way.

The police lab also examined the clothesline used to bind Hartnell and Shepard for clues. They removed the car door message for testing and handwriting analysis. They also took aerial photos of the crime scene. They interviewed Hartnell, who was able to give police a general description of the man, even though the attacker had been wearing a hooded mask.

HANDWRITING ANALYSIS

Like fingerprints, handwriting is unique for every person. Each writer has his or her own handwriting style. While some people can have a few of the same characteristics, it is impossible for two people to write in exactly the same way. Therefore, forensic scientists can use handwriting analysis to compare a sample of text for which the writer is known and one for which the writer is unknown. They search for differences that will determine if the two documents have different writers. When looking for differences, handwriting analysts look at three things: letter form, line form, and formatting. Letter form includes the curves, slants, and size of letters. Line form includes how smooth and dark the lines are, which indicates the pressure the writer uses. Formatting relates to the spacing between letter and words and the placement of words on a line.

Narlow conferred with Solano County's detective Lundblad and Vallejo's detective Lynch, as well as Mel Nicolai of the California Department of Justice. The four men worked together on the Zodiac case, combing through information and developing theories. They thought about what the three attacks had in common. First, all of the victims were young students or couples. The attacks had all occurred on weekends, and two were near holidays. The attacks all happened at dusk or at night, and all were near remote areas. None of the victims were robbed or sexually assaulted. Each time, a different weapon had been used. In addition, the victims were all killed near or in cars. Finally, the Zodiac seemed to have a need to brag about the murders either via phone calls to police or letters to newspapers. After reviewing all of this evidence, the police were still stumped. Who was the Zodiac killer? For cabdriver Paul Stine, the unanswered question would prove to be deadly.

A Deadly Fare

On October 11, 1969, only a few weeks after the Lake Berryessa attack, cab driver Paul Stine picked up a man in San Francisco. The passenger told Stine to drive to an address in the Presidio Heights neighborhood. When Stine reached the address, the man asked him to drive another block.

When Stine stopped the cab, the man in the back seat pressed a gun against Stine's right cheek, just in front of his right ear. The attacker then wrapped his other arm around Stine's neck. When Stine struggled, the man shot and killed him. The killer then got out of the cab, opened the right front door, and slid into the front seat. He held Stine's head while he took Stine's wallet and tore a piece of his bloody shirt.

PRESIDIO

From 1847 to 1994, the Presidio in San Francisco was a US Army post. Through the twentieth century, the Presidio was an important part of American military power in the Pacific. But in 1994, the army post was closed and the Presidio was transferred to the National Park Service. Today, the Presidio is a national park and an outdoor recreation site with forests, trails, a golf course, and scenic overlooks.

Paul Stine

He attempted to wipe down the cab to remove his fingerprints. Then he walked away, still holding a piece of Stine's shirt.

Eyewitness to Murder

At 9:55 p.m. that night, a 14-year-old girl looked out a second-floor window of her house. Across the street, she saw two men in the front seat of a parked cab. It was too dark for her to see what they were doing, but something seemed strange. The girl called her 16-year-old brother to come to the window. He and a younger brother joined the girl and looked outside. From their position about 50 feet (15 m) away, they could see the strange actions of the man inside the cab.[1] They couldn't tell if the passenger was struggling with the cabbie or searching him. Regardless, it was odd. They called the police.

As the Zodiac killer walked away from the cab, a police car headed to the scene. Officers in the car noticed a stocky white man dressed in dark clothes walking toward the nearby

SNIFFING OUT THE KILLER

When police were called to the scene of Paul Stine's murder, they believed the killer would be hiding nearby. They brought special patrol dogs to help them search the area and find where the killer was hiding. These canines were among the best search dogs in the county. They gathered at the front entrance to the Presidio. Officers deployed the search dogs one at a time in different directions. For more than an hour, the search dogs sniffed the area. They sniffed the ground, shrubs, and trees. They checked the surrounding blocks for any person hiding in a doorway, driveway, or other shadowy area. They found nothing.

Presidio area. However, the police dispatcher had made a mistake, identifying the suspect as an African American man. The officers drove by the white man without stopping him. By the time they realized their mistake, the Zodiac had vanished once again.

Crime Scene Investigation

Stine was pronounced dead at the scene. San Francisco homicide inspector Dave Toschi and his partner Bill Armstrong, another homicide inspector, arrived at the crime scene, where they talked to police officers. In a yellow notebook, Toschi took notes. He wrote a description of the body and the crime scene. He sketched the scene, noting the positions of the taxi, the houses, and the body. He made exact measurements with a measuring tape and noted them on his sketch. Armstrong

FINGERPRINT ANALYSIS

The crime lab examiners use a method called ACE-V (analysis, comparison, evaluation, and verification) when examining fingerprints found at a crime scene. First, they analyze a recovered print and determine if it is in good enough condition to be used for a comparison. If it is, then an analyst compares the crime scene print with prints from a suspect. Examining two prints side by side, the analyst compares tiny characteristics and details to determine if the prints match. The examiner evaluates if the two prints are from the same person, if they are from two different people, or if they are inconclusive. Once a decision is made, another examiner independently goes through the entire process to verify the original examiner's results.

took the names and addresses of the witnesses. He had officers check to see if any of the residents had seen or heard anything.

Investigators from the crime lab joined the detectives at the scene. They recovered one 9 mm bullet casing. They dusted the cab for fingerprints. Any prints they found would have to be compared to Stine's prints. They would also have to be compared against the prints of any customers Stine had driven that day. Any prints that could not be matched to Stine or another passenger might belong to the killer. As they searched the inside of the cab, the investigators made an important discovery. They found a print of a right hand made in blood. It had to belong to either Stine or his killer. When the results from the crime lab came back, the blood print did not match Stine's. It belonged to the killer.

Sketching the Killer

Meanwhile, police wanted the children who had seen Stine's killer from the window to help create a sketch of the man. A police sketch artist met with the teens. The teens described the man they had seen as stocky, about five foot, eight inches (1.72 m) tall, wearing a dark jacket and trousers.

A few days after the original sketch of the Zodiac killer suspect was made, the three teen witnesses requested the sketch be changed to make it more accurate, and a second version was made.

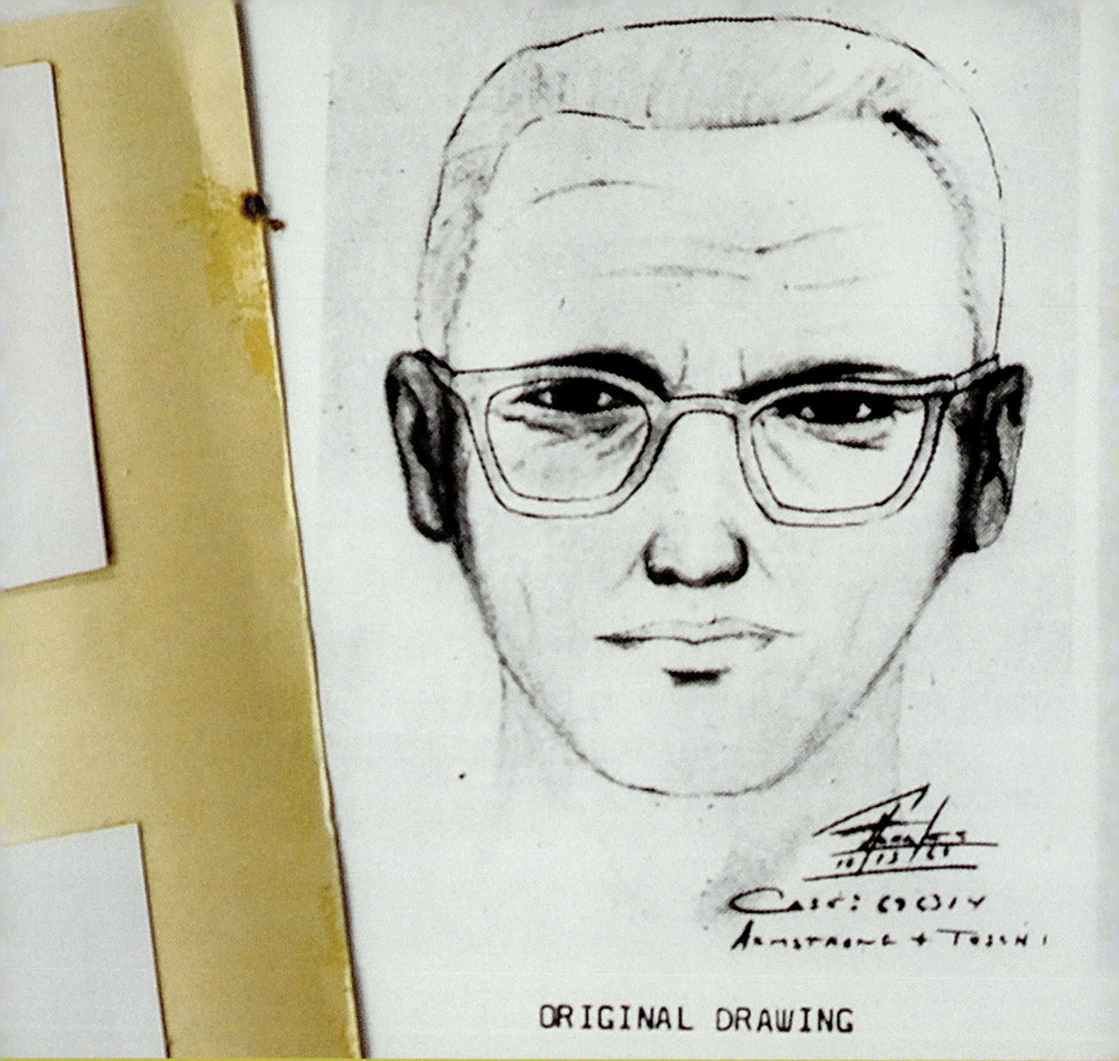

Witnesses to Paul Stine's murder helped police produce their first sketches of a man believed to be the Zodiac killer.

The artist asked them questions about the shape of the man's head, forehead, eyes, nose, ears, and hair. He created a sketch of the suspect based on their answers. When the drawing was complete, Toschi and Armstrong sent it to each cab company in the city to ask drivers to be on the lookout. They asked for any driver who had seen a person resembling the sketch to call the police.

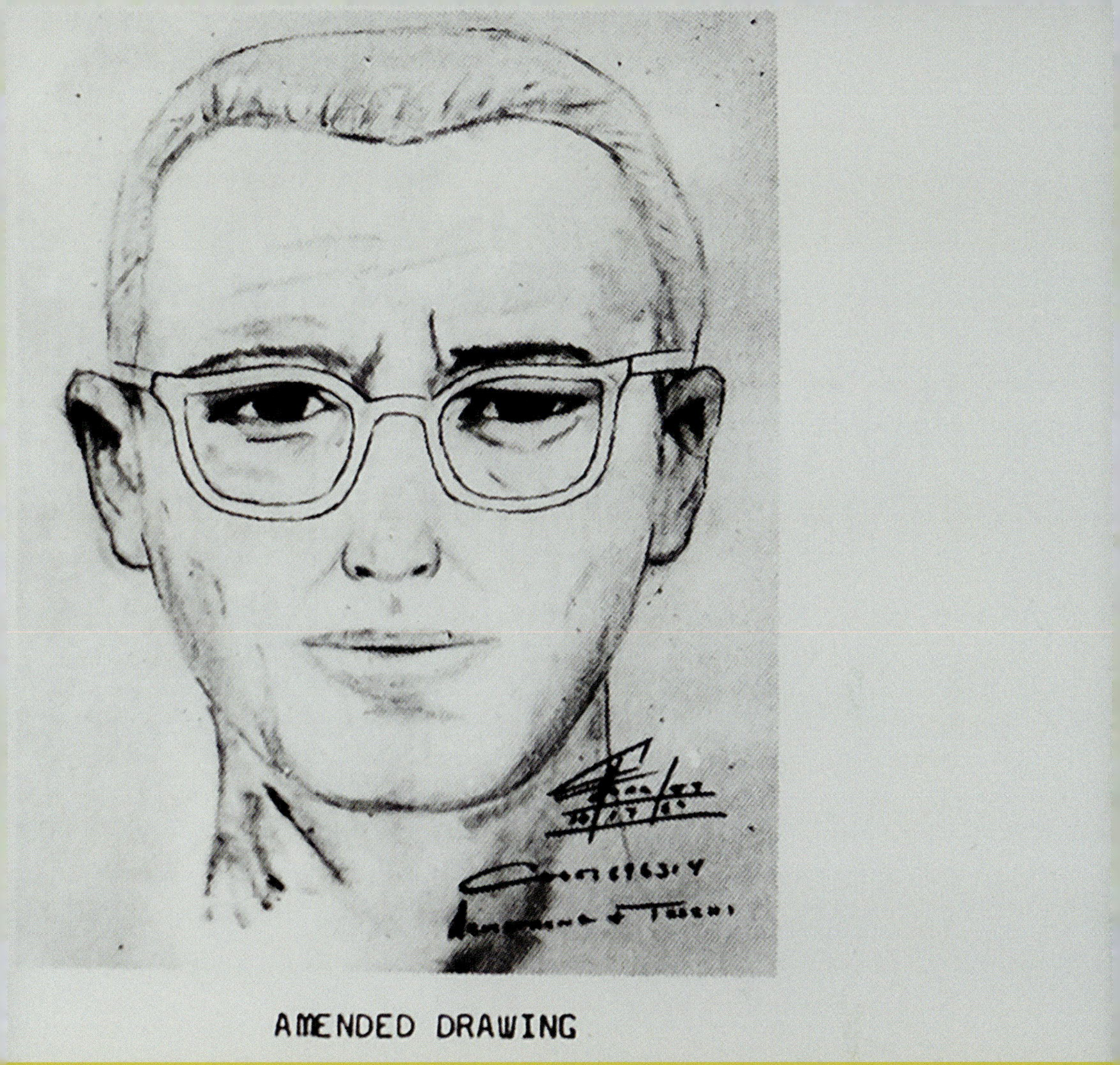

Toschi and Armstrong did not immediately realize that the Zodiac killer had murdered Stine. They believed it was a cab robbery that had turned violent. However, they soon learned this was not a simple robbery. On October 14, a letter arrived at the *Chronicle*. In it, the Zodiac confessed to the cab driver's murder.

CHAPTER SIX

MORE LETTERS FROM THE ZODIAC

Like the letters before it, the October 14, 1969, letter from the Zodiac to the *Chronicle* had a message written on the outside of its envelope: "Please Rush to Editor."[1] This letter was also postmarked from San Francisco. Instead of including a return address, the sender had drawn a circle with a cross, the symbol of the Zodiac killer.

A Letter and a Threat

Inside the envelope, there was a folded letter. This time, the Zodiac included something else, too. The *Chronicle* editor pulled out a small piece of cloth. It was neatly torn, not cut. And it was spattered with blood.

In the letter, the Zodiac claimed responsibility for Stine's murder. The letter read, "This is the Zodiac speaking. I am the murderer of the taxi driver over by Washington St & Maple

The Zodiac killed five people in four attacks. Faraday, Jensen, Ferrin, Shepard, and Stine were murdered. Mageau and Hartnell survived.

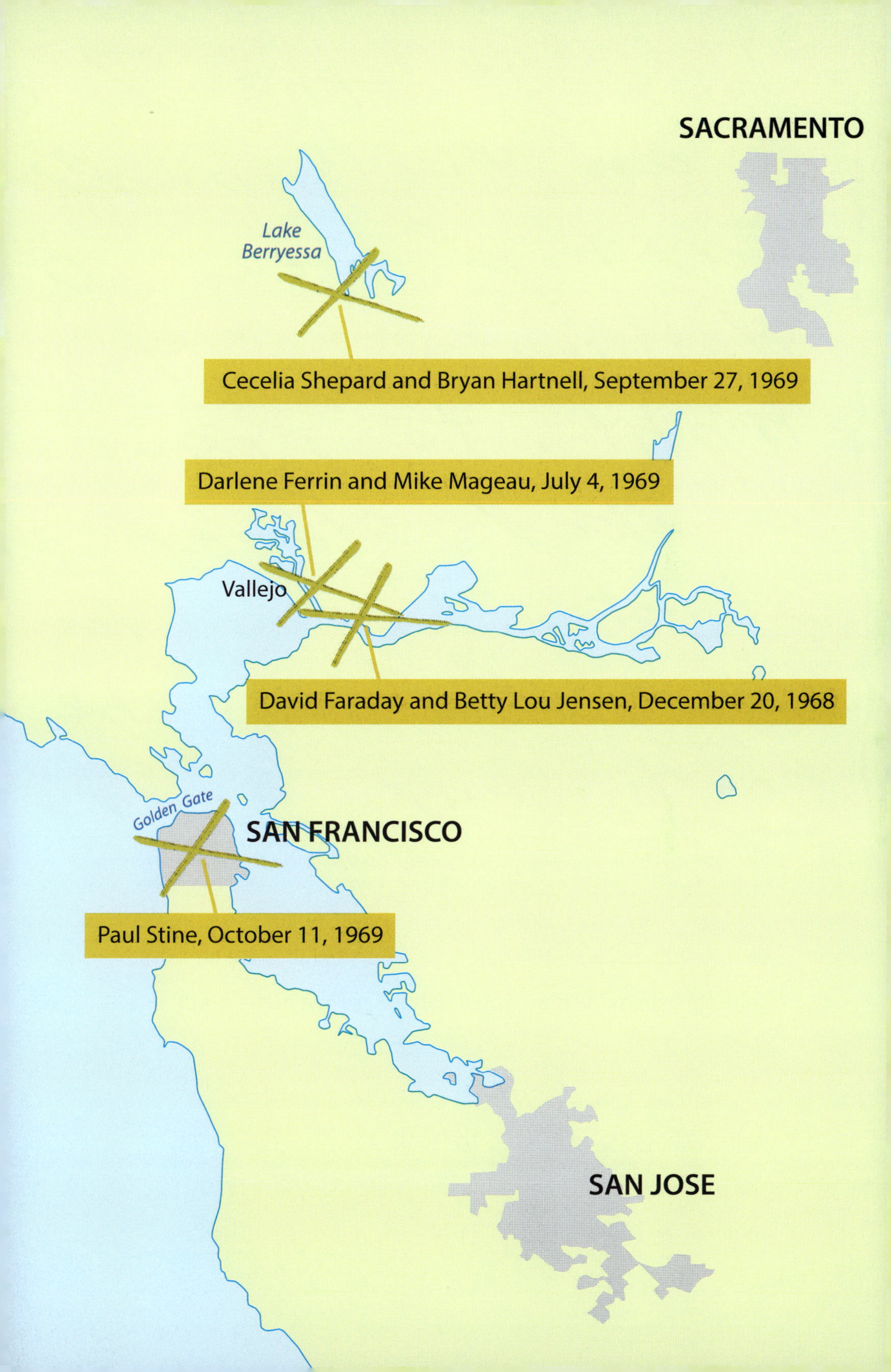

SACRAMENTO
Lake Berryessa
Cecelia Shepard and Bryan Hartnell, September 27, 1969
Darlene Ferrin and Mike Mageau, July 4, 1969
Vallejo
David Faraday and Betty Lou Jensen, December 20, 1968
Golden Gate
SAN FRANCISCO
Paul Stine, October 11, 1969
SAN JOSE

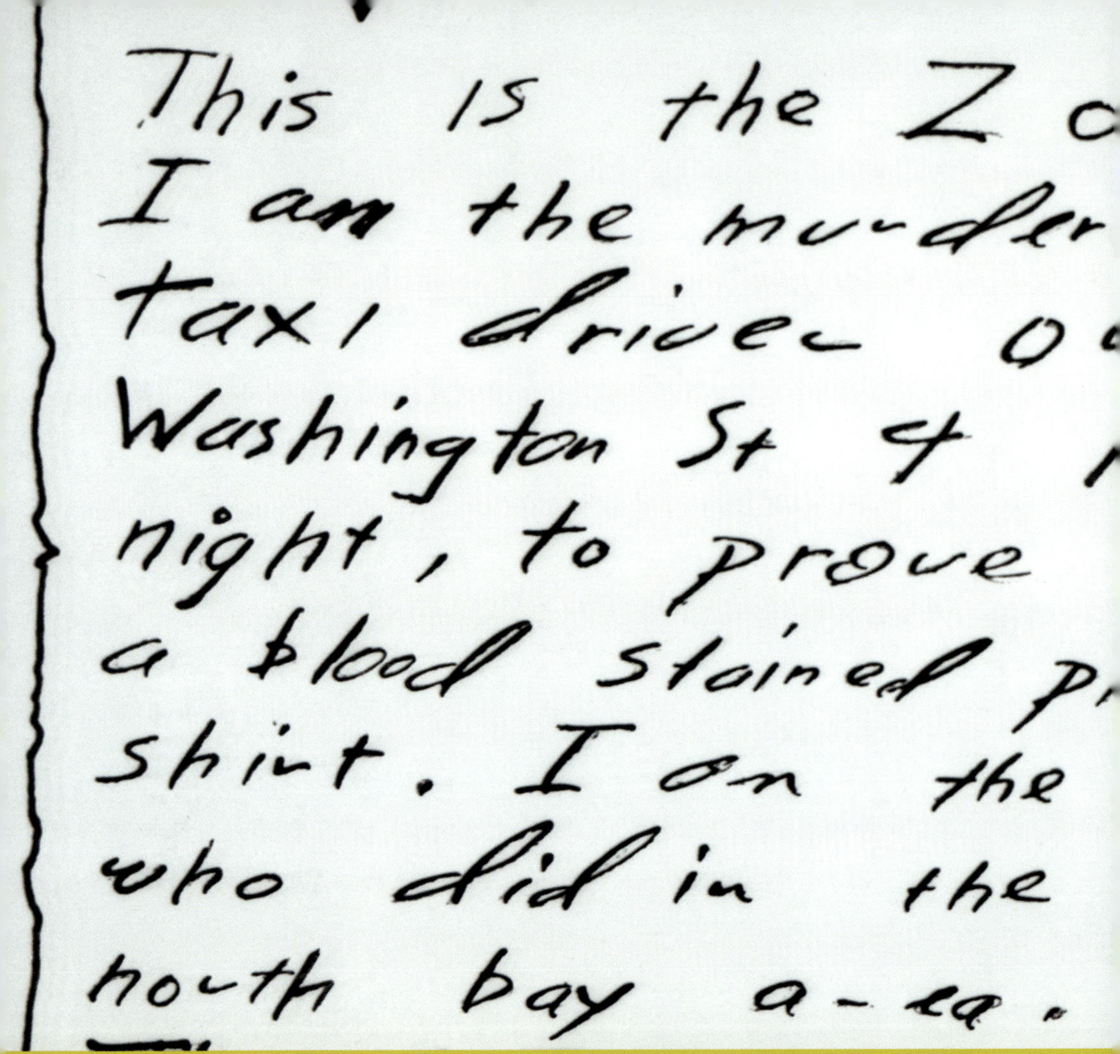
This is the Z
I am the murder
taxi driver o
Washington St &
night, to prove
a blood stained p
shirt. I am the
who did in the
north bay area.

In a letter to the *San Francisco Chronicle*, the Zodiac killer said he killed taxi driver Paul Stine.

St last night, to prove this here is a blood stained piece of his shirt. I am the same man who did in the people in the north bay area."[2]

The Zodiac then taunted the police. He wrote, "The S.F. Police could have caught me last night if they had searched the park properly instead of holding road races with their motorcicles seeing who could make the most noise. The car

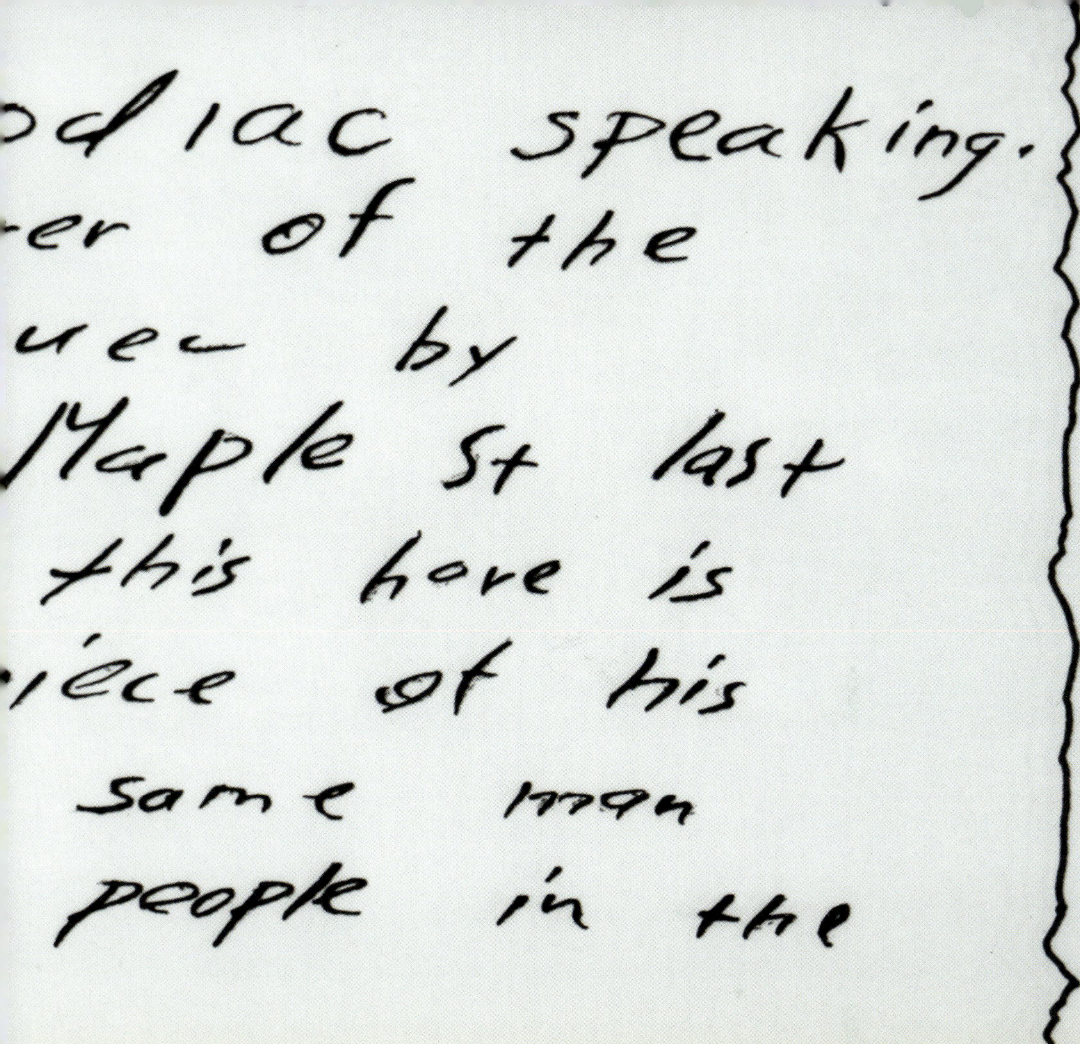
odiac speaking.
er of the
uer by
Maple St last
this here is
iece of his
same man
people in the

drivers should have just parked their cars & sat there quietly waiting for me to come out of cover."[3]

Perhaps the most disturbing part of the letter, however, came in a threat at the end. He wrote, "School children make nice targets, I think I shall wipe out a school bus some morning. Just shoot out the front tire & then pick off the kiddies as they come bouncing out."[4]

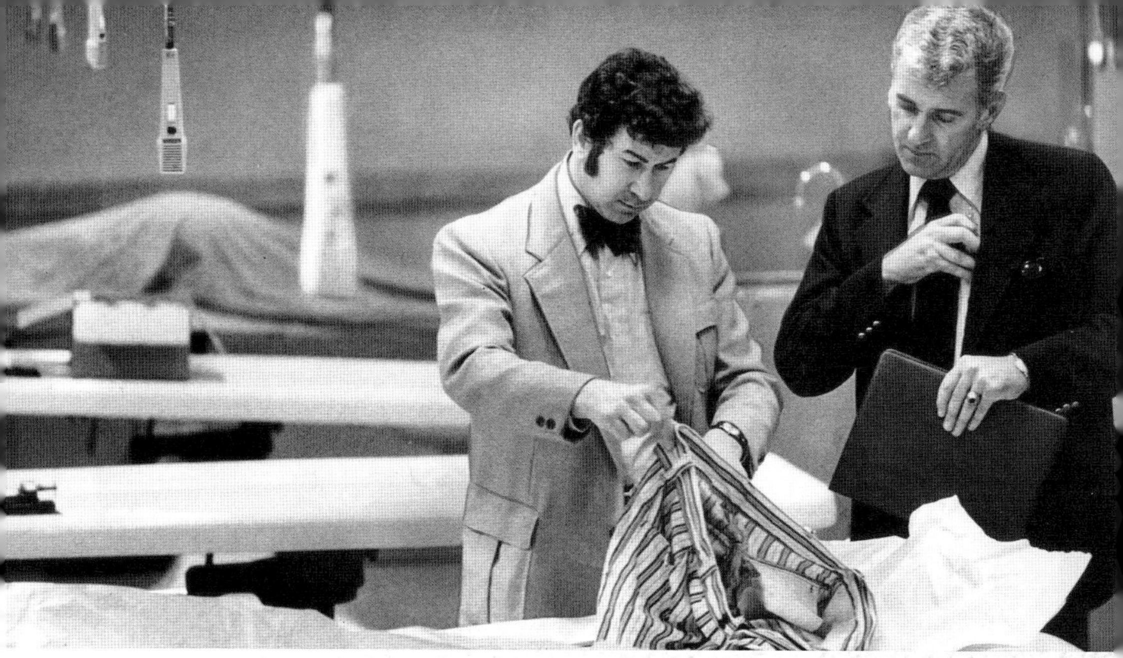

Detectives Toschi, *left*, and Armstrong examine a murder victim's clothing.

The newspaper staff immediately called the San Francisco police. When Detective Toschi saw the bloody piece of shirt, he recognized it as part of Stine's shirt. The police sent the letter to the crime lab to see if any latent prints could be found. The lab sprayed both sides of the letter with a purple chemical solution. If there was any sweat or amino acids left by fingers on the paper, the chemical would react and reveal them.

Toschi and Armstrong compared the bloody cloth to Stine's shirt. It was a match. Next, they compared the handwriting on the latest Zodiac letter with the letters he had sent earlier. Toschi and Armstrong met with other investigators who had been working on the Zodiac murders. After studying the different letters, they agreed that the printing on the newest letter matched those previously sent by the Zodiac.

A Community on Alert

At first, the police asked the newspapers to withhold the Zodiac's threat against schoolchildren as they did not want to start a public panic. By Friday, October 17, they decided to warn the public. They issued an emergency bulletin to all police and school superintendents in the area. In reaction to the bulletin, school bus drivers were instructed what to do if an attack happened. Armed policemen rode on many school buses in Napa Valley to guard them. Other officers patrolled the streets and followed the buses as they picked up and dropped off children. Planes from the Napa Aero Club and the sheriff's department flew over the school bus routes and kept an eye out for any threat.

Meanwhile, the two officers who had seen the man walking near the Presidio on the night of Stine's murder realized that

THE ZODIAC'S VOICE?

On October 22, 1969, a man called the Oakland Police Department and claimed to be the Zodiac. He asked the police operator to get in touch with F. Lee Bailey or Melvin Belli, well-known defense lawyers at the time. He agreed to call in to a San Francisco morning television show if one of the lawyers appeared on the show. By the next morning, Belli appeared on A.M. San Francisco. The show went on the air at 6:30 a.m. At 7:10 a.m., the phone rang. A caller claiming to be the Zodiac spoke a few words and then hung up. Over the next two hours, the man called in to the show 54 times, each time speaking for a few minutes and then hanging up. Belli arranged for the caller to surrender in Daly City later that morning, but the caller claiming to be the Zodiac never showed up.

he may have been the killer. They sat with sketch artists, who created a second drawing of the Zodiac. The new drawing showed a man about 35 to 45 years old, with a thick jaw. He weighed 200 pounds (90 kg) or more and was described as about five feet, eight or nine inches (1.72 to 1.75 m) tall. He had reddish-brown hair in a crew cut and wore heavy rimmed glasses.

Tips Flood Police

By mail and phone, frightened citizens flooded the San Francisco Police Department with tips on possible suspects. The police sorted through thousands of tips that named neighbors, ex-husbands, and coworkers as the Zodiac killer. Throughout Northern California, fear ran high that the Zodiac was on the loose and ready to kill again.

On Sunday, October 19, State Attorney General Thomas C. Lynch issued a public plea for the Zodiac to turn himself in to police. At the same time, he gathered representatives from different police departments and districts to talk about the Zodiac and share information and ideas. Toschi and Armstrong attended the seminar. At the end, they were not any closer to identifying the Zodiac.

In November 1969, the *Chronicle* received two more letters from the Zodiac. Both were postmarked from San Francisco. One had been mailed on November 8, while the other was

THE *EXAMINER* ISSUES A PLEA

On October 19, 1969, the *San Francisco Examiner* printed its own message to the Zodiac killer. It began, "Five people are dead. Let there be no more killings. Police say you are intelligent. If you are, then listen to reason. You are being hunted everywhere in the state and nation. You are alone in this world. You can share your secrets with no one. No friend can help you."

The message also asked the killer to turn himself in: "We offer you no protection, and no sympathy. But we do offer you fair treatment, the assurance of medical help and the full benefits of your legal rights. And we offer to tell your story."[7] The Zodiac killer never responded to this message. And he never wrote again to the *Examiner*.

mailed on November 9. As was the case with the previous letters, "Please Rush to Editor" was written on the envelopes.[5] Once again, the Zodiac had written the letters in small, neat print. This generic writing style made it more difficult for the police to trace him through his handwriting, yet there was no doubt that the letters were from the Zodiac killer. He had included another piece of Stine's shirt in one of the envelopes.

One of the letters was a greeting card with a drawing of a dripping-wet fountain pen on the front. It became known as the "Dripping Pen" letter.[6] Within an hour of receiving the card, police began to check stores that sold greeting cards in hopes of finding a salesperson who remembered selling the card. By this time, there were 50 officers and ten inspectors assigned full-time to the Zodiac case in San Francisco. But the search for a witness was unsuccessful.

A New Cryptogram

In the Dripping Pen letter, the Zodiac included a new cryptogram. It was made of 340 symbols arranged in a block of 20 lines. He signed it with his crossed circle symbol. Toschi photocopied the new cryptogram and sent it to the NSA and the CIA. The *Chronicle* also ran a photo of the cryptogram in the paper, hoping that amateur codebreakers might solve it. However, the cipher was too complex. Even a linguistics expert who ran it through a computer many times was unable to solve it. As of 2019, it was still unsolved.

In the second letter, the Zodiac included a plan for making a bomb. He also drew a diagram of the bomb. He said it would explode at the height of a bus but let cars that were lower to the ground pass by safely. The Zodiac explained that he was storing the bomb in his basement. The police consulted US Army experts to see if the bomb, as described by the Zodiac, could actually be made. A bomb expert said it was possible. The San Francisco police chief then ordered officers to not disclose any details about the bomb. In cooperation with the police, the *Chronicle* agreed not to print any part of the letter that involved the bomb.

The Zodiac sent a total of four cryptograms to newspapers. Only one was solved.

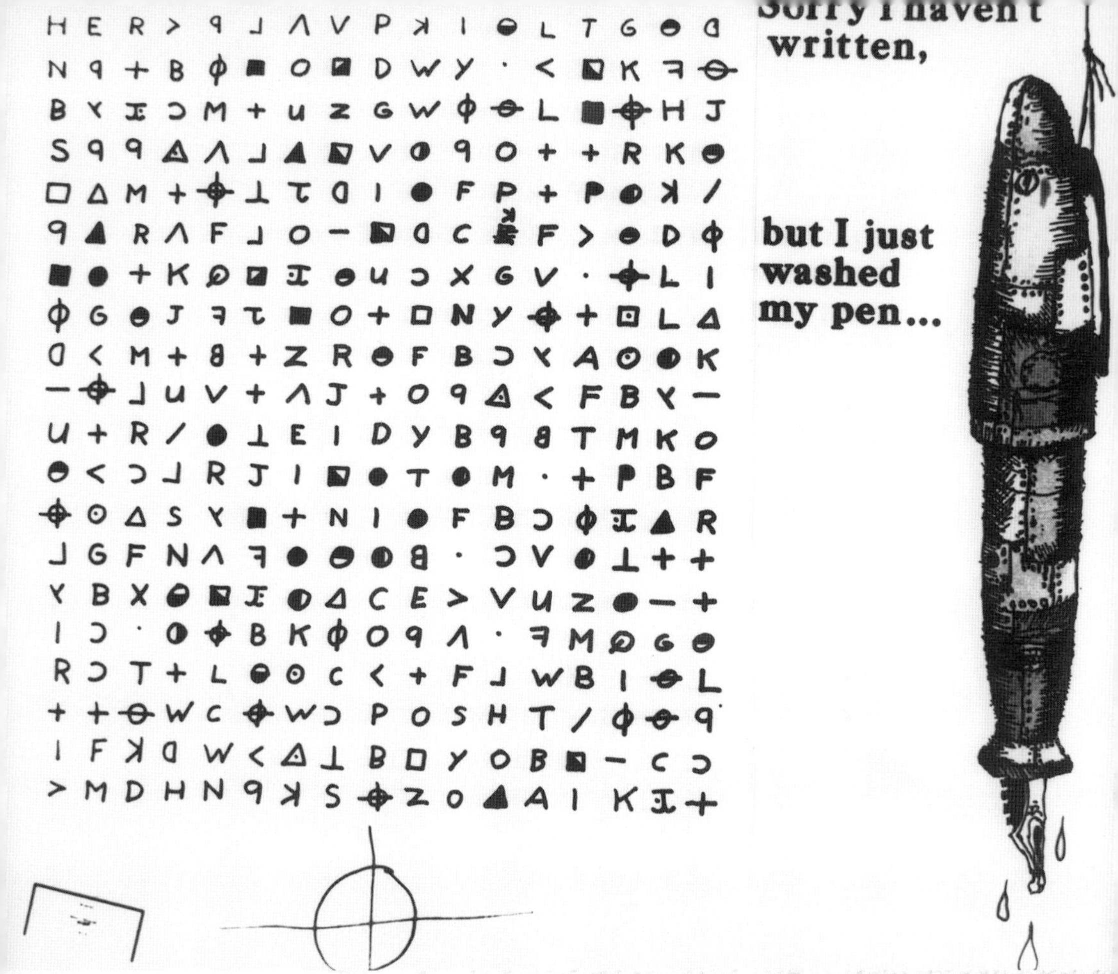

The Zodiac killer sent the Dripping Pen letter to the *San Francisco Chronicle* on November 8, 1969.

The Zodiac's November 9 letter also said that he had killed more people. It began, "This is the Zodiac speaking up to the end of Oct I have killed 7 people."[8] At the time, police had only linked five murders to the Zodiac, yet now he claimed to have killed seven people. Police did not know what to believe. They did not have any unsolved murders they thought could be linked to the Zodiac. Had he really killed two more people? And when would he strike again?

CHAPTER SEVEN

A HIGHWAY ABDUCTION

On March 22, 1970, young mother Kathleen Johns bundled up her ten-month-old daughter, Jennifer, and loaded her into the station wagon. Pregnant with her second child, Johns left her home in San Bernardino, California, at about seven o'clock in the evening and drove toward Petaluma to visit her sick mother. As Johns drove on California Highway 132 through Modesto around 11:15 p.m., she noticed a light-colored car in her rearview mirror.

Car Trouble

Johns slowed down to let the car pass her. Suddenly, the driver blinked his lights and honked his horn. Johns ignored it, hoping the driver would pass and go on his way. Instead, the driver sped up and pulled into the lane next to Johns's station wagon.

Johns was driving on California Highway 132, near Modesto, when she noticed a car following her.

The man yelled through his open passenger-side window that her left rear wheel was wobbling.

Johns was reluctant to stop her car on the deserted road at night with a stranger. She kept driving until she got to a busier road and then pulled over near Interstate 5. The man in the light-colored car parked on the road's shoulder behind the station wagon, got out of his car, and walked over to Johns. He was clean-shaven and neatly dressed. He looked about 30 years old.

The man again told Johns that her left rear wheel was wobbling. He offered to tighten it for her. Johns stayed in the car while the man worked on the wheel, out of her sight. A short time later, he stood up and told her the wheel was fixed. He waved and returned to his car. The man pulled out onto the freeway and drove off.

Ready to continue her trip, Johns pulled back onto the road. She drove only a few car lengths before her entire left rear tire fell off and rolled to the side of the road. She pulled over and got out of the car to see what had happened. Meanwhile, the man noticed what had happened to Johns's car. He returned and offered to drive her to the nearest service station.

Johns could see the lights from a gas station down the road. She lifted Jennifer from the station wagon and got into the man's car. Then she realized that she had left her car's lights on with the keys in the ignition. The man walked back to the station wagon, turned off the lights, and slid the keys into his pocket. With Johns and her baby, the man drove off.

Trapped on a Deserted Road

The man passed the service station without stopping. At first, Johns didn't think anything of it. However, when the man passed the next exit without stopping, she began to get a sinking feeling that something was wrong. Still, she didn't say anything. They traveled past several more exits on the highway, stopping at none.

Then the man turned off the highway and down a deserted farm road. Johns knew she was in trouble. Upset, she asked if he always helped people stranded on the road in this way. The man gave a chilling answer. "When I get through with them they don't need any help," he said.[1] They drove for another

EYEWITNESS ACCURACY

Johns was one of the only people to survive an up-close encounter with an attacker who was likely the Zodiac. Police had hoped her eyewitness testimony would help them uncover his identity. But how accurate is eyewitness testimony? While eyewitness accounts are helpful to investigators, these accounts can often be inaccurate. Two people who view the same event may have different accounts, depending on their position, line of sight, and other conditions that may affect their perception and memory. In addition, how an eyewitness recalls an event may change over time.

30 minutes in the dark. Then the man looked at Johns and said, "You know you're going to die. You know I'm going to kill you."[2]

Johns was terrified. Yet she stayed calm and tried to figure out a way to escape. They drove through backcountry roads, during which time the man rarely spoke, except to promise that he was going to kill her. Johns desperately tried to commit everything about the man to memory, from his shoes and clothes to his face. If she lived, she wanted to be able to give a complete description to police. She thought that he weighed about 170 pounds (77 kg) and was about five foot, nine inches (1.75 m) tall. He wore a black or dark-blue windbreaker and black wool pants. He had black thick-rimmed glasses held in place by an elastic band around his head.

BURNED CAR, BURNED EVIDENCE

Police had hoped they would be able to collect evidence from Johns's car. If her abductor had worked on her tire, he must have left some fingerprints or other evidence behind that could lead to his identification. However, when police returned to Johns's car, they found the car had been set on fire. It was completely burned, and the interior was gutted. The fire destroyed any potential evidence that police could have used to solve the case.

A Daring Escape

Suddenly, Johns saw her chance to escape. The man had mistakenly driven up a freeway off-ramp. When he stopped to turn around, Johns clutched her baby tightly and jumped from the car. She raced across the road and jumped into a ditch surrounded by tall grass. She lay as flat as she could and used her body to muffle any noise the baby might make. With her heart pounding, Johns hid as the man shined a flashlight over the field, searching for her. He called for her to come back to the car. As he stepped forward, a semitruck pulled up. The driver got out of the truck and asked if anything was wrong. The man did not respond. Instead, he jumped into his car and drove away.

Terrified, Johns refused to go with the truck driver and waited with him until a female driver stopped and drove her to the nearest police station. Inside, Johns told a sergeant her story. As she gave her statement, Johns's eyes skimmed the wall where the police had hung their "wanted" posters, which

WAS IT REALLY THE ZODIAC?

In the years since Johns's harrowing abduction, there have been some questions raised about who she really met that night. The Zodiac admitted to the abduction in a letter to the press. However, as the abduction had been reported in the news before the Zodiac's letter, it's possible he was simply trying to take credit for another person's crime. Doubters point to inconsistent statements from Johns that night and in subsequent interviews. However, although Johns may not have been accurate in every detail, she was under a tremendous amount of stress that night. Emotional trauma can affect a person's memory, so the trauma Johns suffered may have caused her to confuse some of the details or the sequence of events from that night.

WANTED

SAN FRANCISCO POLICE DEPARTMENT

0-69 WANTED FOR MURDER OCTOBER 18, 196

ORIGINAL DRAWING

AMENDED DRAWING

upplementing our Bulletin 87-69 of October 13, 1969. Additional information has eveloped the above amended drawing of murder suspect known as "ZODIAC".

MA, 35-45 Years, approximately 5'8", Heavy Build, Short Brown Hair, possibly with ed Tint, Wears Glasses. Armed with 9 MM Automatic.

vailable for comparison: Slugs, Casings, Latents, Handwriting.

NY INFORMATION:
nspectors Armstrong & Toschi
omicide Detail
ASE NO. 696314

THOMAS J. CAHILL
CHIEF OF POLICE

The San Francisco Police Department supplied its sketch of the Zodiac killer to law enforcement across the state, which is how Johns spotted the wanted poster at a police station east of San Francisco.

depicted suspects. One sketch jumped out at her. It was the composite drawing of the Zodiac made after Paul Stine's murder. It looked just like the man who had just abducted her.

In his letter taking credit for Johns's abduction, the Zodiac failed to provide details that would have proven he was involved.

In the following days, Detective Toschi sent Johns several confidential photos of suspects. He believed the man who had abducted her and her baby was the Zodiac. Johns had spent more time up close with the Zodiac than any other victim. The Zodiac hadn't been wearing a hood or disguise when he was with her. Toschi hoped that she would finally be the one who could identify the Zodiac. However, Johns did not recognize any of the men in the photos. None were the man who had abducted her that night. Months later, the Zodiac confirmed Toschi's suspicions. In a July 1970 letter to the *Chronicle*, he claimed responsibility for the abduction of Johns and her baby.

CHAPTER EIGHT

WHERE IS THE ZODIAC?

As the Zodiac sent letters and cards to the press in the early 1970s, investigators continued their search for the killer. They followed several leads and even discovered a potential Zodiac connection to a murder in Southern California. However, they were still unable to find the killer himself.

On April 21, 1970, the Zodiac's ninth letter arrived at the *Chronicle*. The newspaper called Detective Toschi, who rushed over to see if the letter was in fact from the Zodiac. Toschi believed the letter was from the Zodiac killer.

Another Cryptogram

In the letter, the Zodiac teased the police with his identity. He wrote, "This is the Zodiac speaking By the way have you cracked the last cipher I sent you? My name is —" followed by

The San Francisco Chronicle continued to receive letters from the Zodiac killer in the early 1970s.

San Francisco Chronicle
BABSON COLLEGE

Officers met frequently to discuss the Zodiac investigation. The case involved investigators from numerous California cities and counties, as well as state law enforcement and federal agencies.

a new 13-character cryptogram.[1] Was this the clue that would finally reveal the Zodiac's identity?

Numerous detectives and code experts studied the 13-character coded message. They tried to look at the symbols in different ways. Three of the symbols were the numeral 8 in a circle. These looked out of place in the cryptogram, as the

Zodiac had never used numbers before in his coded messages. Investigators could not crack the code.

Also in the April 21 letter, the Zodiac drew a diagram of a bomb that he threatened to use to blow up a school bus. At the bottom of the diagram, the Zodiac drew his crossed circle symbol followed by *=10* and *SFPD=0*. Toschi believed this meant

MURDER IN SANTA BARBARA

Although not officially credited to the Zodiac killer, the murder of two high school seniors in 1963 California had many similarities. In June 1963, high school seniors Robert Domingos and Linda Edwards skipped school on "Senior Ditch Day" and went to a beach near Gaviota State Park in Santa Barbara County. When the couple did not come home, Robert's father went to the beach and found the teens bound with rope and dead inside a shack. The victims had been shot multiple times with a .22 caliber weapon. Investigators had few leads on who had murdered the teens. In 1972, the Santa Barbara County Sheriff's Department announced the case might be connected to the Zodiac killings. The beach killer had used the same ammunition that was used in the 1968 murders of David Faraday and Betty Lou Jensen. The beach killing also had several similarities to the Zodiac's 1969 attack at Lake Berryessa.

the Zodiac was claiming he had killed ten people so far.[2] If true, Toschi wondered who the additional unidentified victims were. Police had only linked the Zodiac to five murders. They had no leads on any others, and the Zodiac gave no further clues.

More Letters

A few days later, on April 29, the *Chronicle* received the Zodiac's tenth letter—a greeting card. Again, it was postmarked from San Francisco. Inside the card, the Zodiac wrote, "I hope you enjoy yourselves when I have my Blast," and he drew the crossed circle symbol.[3] On the back of the card, the Zodiac threatened police that he would use the bus bomb unless the *Chronicle* published the full details of his letters. He also asked for people to start wearing Zodiac buttons. No buttons were made.

A few months later, the Zodiac wrote his eleventh letter, postmarked June 26, 1970. The letter said the Zodiac was very upset that he was not seeing the public wearing Zodiac buttons. He claimed to have shot a man in a parked car with a .38. Some suspected that he was referring to the murder of Sergeant Richard Radetich, who had been shot in his squad car a week earlier. However, the San Francisco police denied that this was the work of Zodiac.

This June letter included a roadmap of the San Francisco area. On the map, the Zodiac drew his crossed circle symbol with compass markings. The letter also included a 32-character cryptogram. The Zodiac claimed that together, the coded message and the map led to a bomb that he had buried. However, the coded message was never decrypted, and the alleged bomb was never discovered. The Zodiac ended the letter with his signature of sorts, drawing the crossed circle followed by *=12* and *SFPD=0*. Again, he did not give any specific details about the additional murders that

The Zodiac sent at least 18 letters.[4] He usually sent them to newspapers but occasionally sent letters to private citizens.

he claimed to have committed, and police had not connected any additional cases to the Zodiac.[5]

The *Chronicle* received several more letters from the Zodiac in 1970. One of those letters was a Halloween card sent to *Chronicle* reporter Paul Avery (although the Zodiac misspelled the name as "Averly") in October 1970.[6] Avery was a reporter who had been covering the Zodiac case for the newspaper. The card was signed with a letter Z and the Zodiac's symbol. Handwritten on the front of the card was a threatening message. It read, "Peek-a-boo, you are doomed!"[7] Shortly after receiving the Halloween card, Avery received an anonymous letter mailed from Southern California. The letter suggested that the Zodiac may have started his killing spree in Southern California. The anonymous writer pointed to similarities between the Zodiac's murders and the unsolved 1966 murder of Cheri Jo Bates, a student at Riverside Community College.

The Case of Cheri Jo Bates

Upon receiving this letter, Avery contacted the Riverside police and spoke with Captain Irv Cross. Cross told him that there was a man who had been trying to convince the Riverside police that the Zodiac was responsible for Bates's murder. Cross believed this local man had written the anonymous letter to Avery. Cross outlined the case to Avery and promised to send information from the case file as soon as possible. At first,

Cheri Jo Bates was murdered in Riverside, three years before the first attack officially credited to the Zodiac killer and hundreds of miles south of where the confirmed Zodiac killings occurred. But some people believe the Zodiac killed Bates, too.

Avery doubted that the Bates killing and the Zodiac murders were connected. Cheri Jo Bates was an 18-year-old college freshman at Riverside Community College. On October 30, 1966, she disappeared after going to the campus library. Her body was found the next day, brutally beaten and stabbed. About a month later, the Riverside police and the local newspaper received nearly identical typed letters titled "The Confession."[8] The author claimed to be the killer and gave details of the murder that had not been released publicly. In the letter, the writer warned, "She is not the first and she will not be the last."[9] The writer insisted that the letter be published in the newspaper.

Six months after the murder, the Riverside police received another letter. In large writing, it said that Bates had to die and warned that there would be more killings. At the bottom of the paper, the killer had drawn what looked like a small letter Z.[10]

The Zodiac eventually claimed he had 37 victims total, though law enforcement only counts seven (five killed, two injured) to be confirmed Zodiac victims.[12]

Avery also reviewed a photo of a desktop discovered at the Riverside campus library five months after the murder. A gruesome poem about death and spilling blood had been written on the desk in blue pen. It was signed with two lowercase letters, *r* and *h*.[11]

ZODIAC IN NEW YORK

The search for leads in the Zodiac case led police from California to Albany, New York. The *Albany Times Union* newspaper received a letter postmarked on August 1, 1973. In place of a return address, the sender had drawn the symbol of the Zodiac killer. The letter inside taunted that the writer was not dead or in the hospital and threatened to start killing again. The writer included a three-line coded message that he said revealed the name and location of his next victim. Analysts decrypted the message to read "Albany Medical Center. This is only the beginning."[14] Yet police could not link any murders in the area to the letter. Handwriting experts could not verify if the letter had been written by the writer of the Zodiac letters, but neither could they rule out the possibility.

Avery noted that the printing on the Bates note and the desktop poem were similar to the lettering in the Zodiac's recent letters to the *Chronicle*. Avery consulted with Sherwood Morrill, a handwriting expert for the California Department of Justice. After careful examination, Morrill said that he believed the Riverside letters were almost certainly the work of the Zodiac. Although he had his doubts at the beginning, Avery agreed.

In November 1970, Avery wrote an article for the *Chronicle* about his investigation of the link between the Riverside murder and the Zodiac case. Five months later, the Zodiac mailed another letter, this time to the *Los Angeles Times*. In the letter, he gave credit to the police for discovering that he had killed someone in Riverside. However, he taunted them, saying, "They are only finding the easy ones, there are . . . a lot more."[13]

THE ZODIAC'S LETTERS

1969

AUGUST 1, 1969

- The first three Zodiac letters are received by the *San Francisco Chronicle*, the *San Francisco Examiner*, and the *Vallejo Times-Herald*. Each contains one-third of the Zodiac's first cryptogram. The letters also claim credit for the murders of David Faraday, Betty Lou Jensen, and Darlene Ferrin.

AUGUST 4, 1969

- In a three-page letter to the *Examiner*, the killer calls himself by the name Zodiac for the first time.

OCTOBER 14, 1969

- The *Chronicle* receives a Zodiac letter containing part of Paul Stine's shirt. In the letter, the Zodiac claims credit for Stine's murder and threatens to attack a school bus.

NOVEMBER 8, 1969

- The Zodiac sends the "Dripping Pen" letter to the *Chronicle* with a new cryptogram.

NOVEMBER 9, 1969

- The Zodiac sends a letter to the *Chronicle* that includes a plan for a bomb.

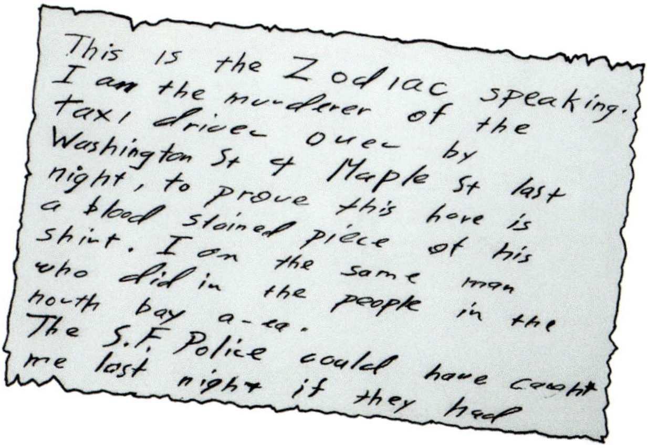
This is the Zodiac speaking.
I am the mu-derer of the
taxi drive- ove- by
Washington St + Maple St last
night, to prove this here is
a blood stained piece of his
shi-t. I am the same man
who did in the people in the
north bay a-ea.
The S.F. Police could have caught
me last night if they had

1970

APRIL 21, 1970
- The *Chronicle* receives a Zodiac letter with a new cryptogram.

APRIL 28, 1970
- In a letter to the *Chronicle*, the Zodiac asks the public to wear Zodiac buttons.

JUNE 26, 1970
- The Zodiac sends another cryptogram to the *Chronicle*.

JULY 24, 1970
- In a letter to the *Chronicle*, the Zodiac claims credit for the abduction of Kathleen Johns.

OCTOBER 27, 1970
- The Zodiac sends a Halloween card to *Chronicle* reporter Paul Avery.

1971

MARCH 13, 1971
- The Zodiac mails a letter to the *Los Angeles Times* in which he claims credit for the murder of Cheri Jo Bates.

1974

JANUARY 29, 1974
- The Zodiac sends a letter to the *Chronicle* referencing the movie *The Exorcist*.

These are some of the letters the Zodiac killer sent between 1969 and the early 1970s. There are 18 confirmed Zodiac letters, and others that claim to be from the Zodiac but are likely copycats.

Although some people believe that Cheri Jo Bates is one of the Zodiac's victims, the police have never officially connected Bates's murder to the Zodiac killer. Some believe that even though another person may have committed the murder, the Zodiac tried to take credit for Bates's death.

The Zodiac Goes Silent

Between March 1971 and January 1974, the Zodiac went silent. No one knew what had happened to him or where he had gone. Was he dead? Had he been locked up in prison or a mental institution? No one knew. And they were still no closer to discovering who he was. As fewer leads came in, law enforcement agencies began pulling their investigators off the Zodiac case, turning their attention to other crimes. By the mid-1970s, only Detective Toschi remained assigned to the Zodiac case. With no new developments in the case, the public's interest in the Zodiac killer diminished.

1978 LETTER—REAL OR FAKE?

In April 1978, the *San Francisco Chronicle* received another letter from someone claiming to be the Zodiac. The letter arrived four years after the last confirmed communication from the Zodiac killer. While some people believed the letter to be real, others thought it was a hoax. Some suspected Detective Toschi was the author. They believed he faked the letter to keep the story of the Zodiac killer alive in the media. Toschi was suspended from the police department that July, and he was investigated. Eventually, he was cleared of forging the Zodiac letter, but he was removed from the Zodiac case. Toschi retired from the police force in 1987 and died in 2018 at age 86.

On January 29, 1974, a new letter from the Zodiac arrived. The letter mentioned the horror movie *The Exorcist*, which had been released in theaters in December 1973. This movie reference made police believe that the Zodiac was still alive. In 1974, the Zodiac mailed four letters to the *Chronicle*. After that, he went silent again. Over the years, some similar letters have been sent to the press, claiming to be from the Zodiac, but none have been verified. It is widely believed that these letters were from copycats.

By 1981, the Zodiac killer case was cold. The San Francisco Police Department turned the case over to the California Department of Justice in Sacramento, California. The Zodiac—who officials believe killed at least five people and who has claimed to have killed more than 30—has never been found.

CHAPTER NINE

IDENTITY UNKNOWN

Two decades into the twenty-first century, the identity of the Zodiac killer is still unknown. Despite all of the evidence collected in the case, the police have never been able to connect it to the killer. They never found the gun or guns used by the Zodiac killer to match shell casings and bullets found at the crime scenes. They could not find a match for the palm print in the pay phone booth or the bloody print in Paul Stine's cab. Although the Zodiac sent pieces of Stine's shirt to the press, the rest of the shirt has never been found. And several of the Zodiac's cryptogram clues have never been solved. "For me, the Zodiac case is the number one unsolved American criminal mystery," said Mark Hewitt, a California-based author who has published a trilogy of books on the Zodiac. "I think there are more people looking into this case than any other case."[1]

A handwriting expert discusses a Zodiac letter at the University of Pittsburgh in 2016. Although the Zodiac has been inactive for years, the case is still examined.

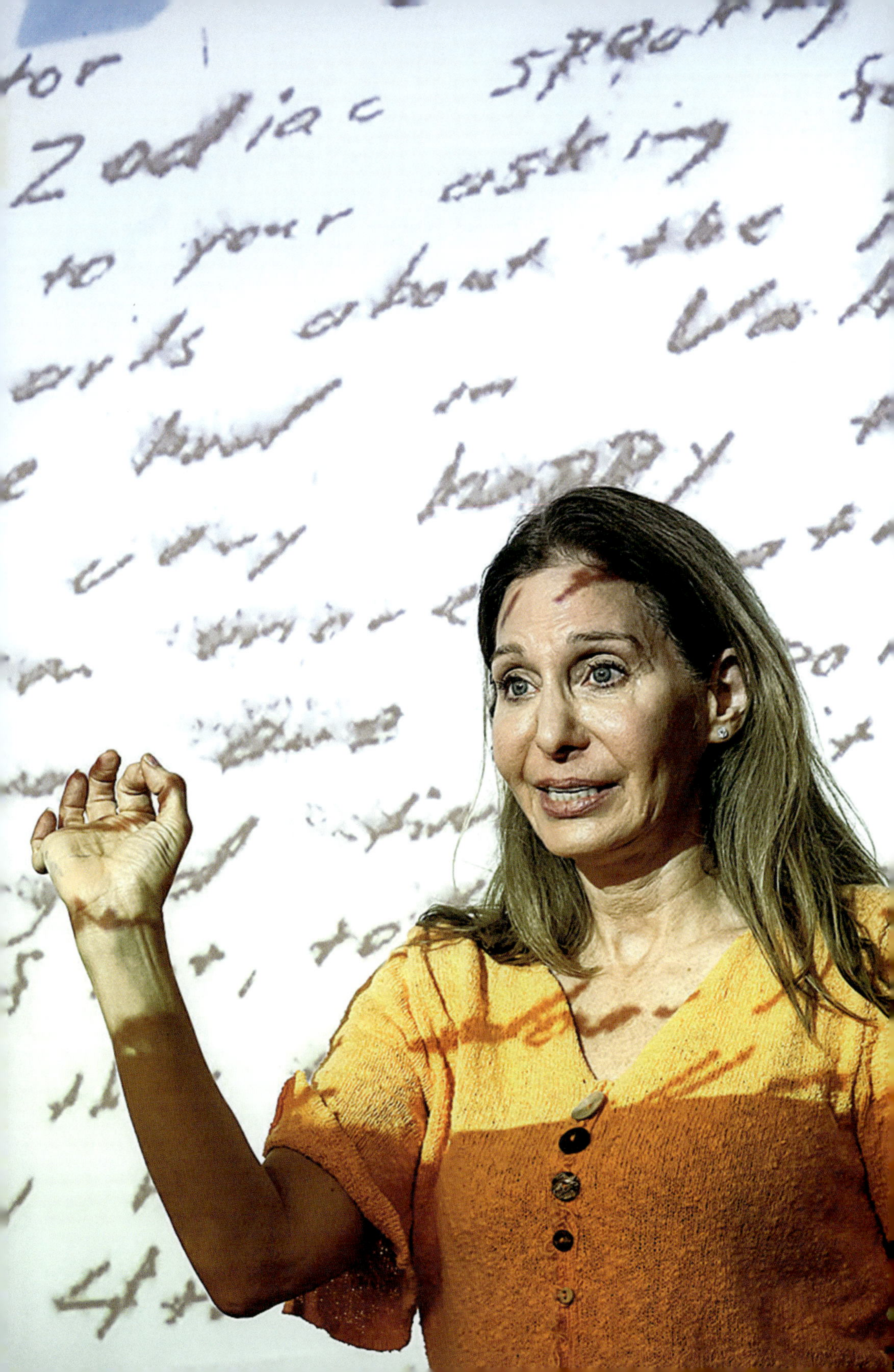
Zodiac
asking
to your
about the

THE ZODIAC KILLER IN POP CULTURE

For years, the public has been fascinated by the unsolved murders claimed by the Zodiac killer. Who was he, and why did he kill? How did he choose his victims? This fascination with the murders and cryptograms has inspired many legends and theories, as well as books, movies, and websites. Scott Bonn is a criminologist and author of the book *Why We Love Serial Killers: The Curious Appeal of the World's Most Savage Murderers*. He believes the public is fascinated with stories about serial killers like the Zodiac killer because they are exciting. "They have a visceral appeal for the public similar to monster movies because they provide a euphoric adrenaline rush. Consequently, their atrocity tales in the news and entertainment media are addictive," he wrote in an article for *Psychology Today* in 2017.[2]

Arthur Leigh Allen

Over the years, police have investigated thousands of leads and suspects in the Zodiac case. All of the suspects were cleared. One of the most promising suspects was Arthur Leigh Allen, a resident of Vallejo and a convicted child molester. Allen owned a Zodiac watch with a crossed-circle symbol similar to the one used by the killer. He also owned boots identical to those worn by the Zodiac. In one interview with police, he said that his favorite short story was *The Most Dangerous Game* by Richard Connell, which the Zodiac killer mentioned in one of his letters. Allen also reportedly confessed to a friend that he was the Zodiac. Years after the murders, Mike Mageau identified him in a photo lineup as the man who had shot him.

Even so, police never had enough evidence to arrest and charge Allen. They compared his fingerprints to those found in Paul Stine's cab, but the prints did not match. Allen died of a heart attack in 1992 at age 58. After his death, some people still believed he was the Zodiac killer. In 2002, forensic analysts compared Allen's DNA to a partial piece of DNA in the saliva on an envelope sent by Zodiac. Although the test was not a match, technology at the time did not allow for a clean sample to be taken from the glue on the envelopes the killer had sent to the press. As a result, some people believe the DNA test was flawed.

There are people who still believe that Allen is guilty. "I believe he did it, no doubt. There are just way too many coincidences that make way too much sense," said John Henslin, a friend of murder victim Betty Lou Jensen.[3]

ZODIAC ON THE BIG SCREEN

In 2007, the movie *Zodiac* starring Mark Ruffalo, Robert Downey Jr., and Jake Gyllenhaal was released. The movie was based on the book *Zodiac* by Robert Graysmith. Graysmith worked at the *San Francisco Chronicle* as a cartoonist while the Zodiac killer was active. The film follows the Zodiac murders and the hunt to find the killer. Reviews of the film were generally positive, and it was nominated for several awards. Audiences flocked to see it, and the film grossed more than $84 million worldwide.[4]

Other Theories

There are many theories about who the Zodiac

THE UNABOMBER

Some people think that Ted Kaczynski, also known as the Unabomber, may have also been the Zodiac killer. A former professor, Kaczynski was arrested in 1996 in Montana for a series of mail bombings that killed three people and injured 24.[5] He was sentenced to life in prison without the possibility of parole. Kaczynski shared some similarities with the Zodiac killer. He lived in the San Francisco area in the late 1960s; he showed the ability to build bombs, and he liked to communicate with the news media after his attacks. However, police and the FBI cleared Kaczynski as a suspect in the Zodiac case because his fingerprints did not match those left by the Zodiac killer.

killer could be. Some people believe he was mentally ill, but his urge to kill lessened in his mid-30s, and he appears to have stopped committing murders. Others think he might be Ted Kaczynski (known as the Unabomber, famous for mailing deadly bombs to people between 1978 and 1995), a gang of cops, or a crazy neighbor.

Dozens of people have come forward to name their fathers or family members as the Zodiac killer. In April 2009, Deborah Perez told the press that her deceased father, Guy Ward Hendrickson, was the Zodiac killer. She claimed she had written some of the letters that her father sent to the press and had embroidered the mask he wore during some of the attacks. She also handed over glasses that she said her father took from cabbie Paul Stine. However, the police determined the glasses did not belong to Stine. Other family members denied that Hendrickson was involved in the Zodiac killings.

In 2014, Gary Stewart wrote a book and claimed that his biological father Earl Van Best Jr. was the Zodiac killer. Van Best, who was dead when the book was published, had a criminal record in San Francisco and also had a strong physical resemblance to the police sketch of the killer. In his book, Stewart presents his father as a boy with disturbing fixations, a frustrated intellectual, and a jilted lover who was unable to control his rage. However, police have found no evidence linking Van Best to the Zodiac murders.

The San Francisco Police Department closed the Zodiac investigation in 2004, the first time in the department's history that it had closed an unsolved homicide investigation. However, the case has since been reopened.

Still Searching

Although it has been more than 50 years since the Zodiac killer first struck, police continue to investigate and hunt down any leads that arise in the case. "We have talked to many people over the years. We've gotten reports over the years from people who don't pan out. This case is still open, and we still do accept tips or leads that may have bearing on the case," said Steve Blower, a retired captain of the Napa County Sheriff's Office.[6]

As forensic science has improved in the years since the Zodiac murders, police hope that advances in DNA technology and genealogy databases may allow them to one day identify the Zodiac killer. In 2018, detectives from the Vallejo Police Department sent two envelopes from letters sent by the Zodiac killer to a private lab for advanced DNA analysis that had not been available years earlier. This was an attempt to obtain DNA from the saliva on the envelope flap and stamps. The police hoped the analysis would provide a genetic profile of the Zodiac killer that could be used to compare to profiles in genealogy websites, which could potentially allow investigators to track down the Zodiac through his family tree. Results of this DNA analysis had not been released to the public as of May 2019.

Using genealogy to track down a killer is a relatively new technique. In previous years, most investigations ran DNA samples through state and federal databases that held DNA from convicted criminals. To find a match, the DNA had to belong to someone who was already convicted of a crime or a close relative of someone who had been convicted and was in the database. In contrast, genealogy databases contain a much wider pool of DNA from people who are searching for relatives and want to learn about their family history. This gives investigators hope that they will be able to use DNA and genealogy to crack the Zodiac case.

In 2018, police arrested 72-year-old Joseph James DeAngelo, whom they believe is the Golden State Killer. The Golden

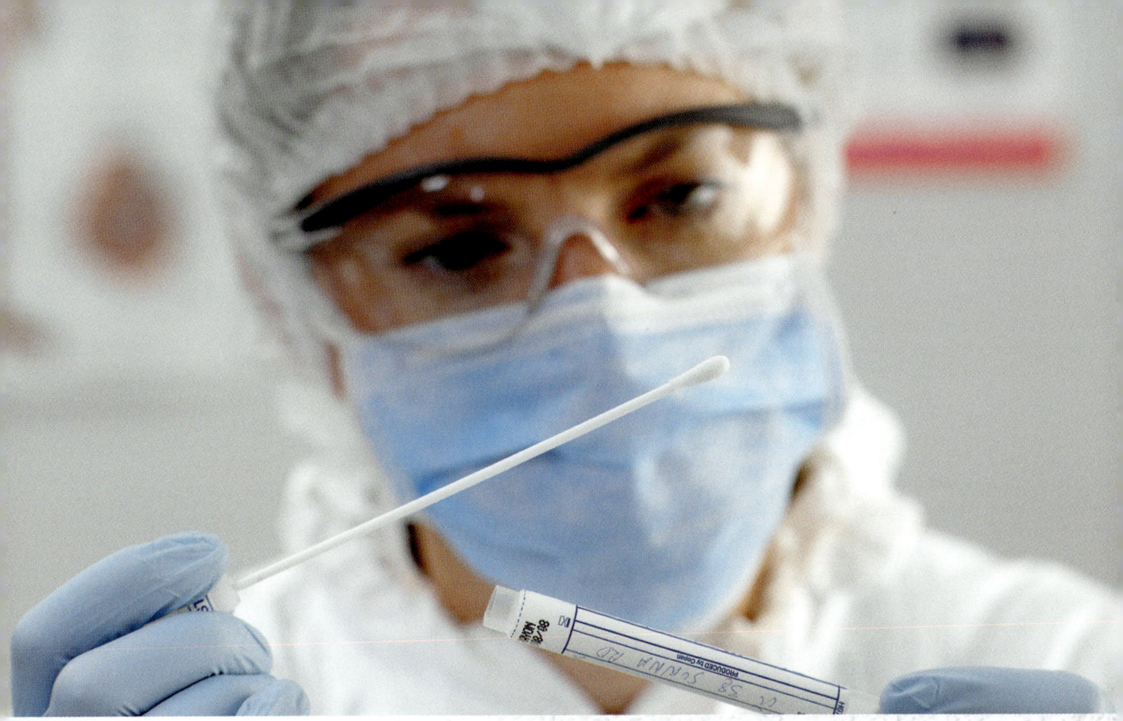

Investigators are hopeful that technological advancements in DNA analysis could eventually help catch the Zodiac killer.

State Killer was linked to more than 50 rapes and 12 murders between 1976 and 1986.[7] However, he had eluded police for decades. Police were able to use a public genealogy website to track him down. They had a well-preserved sample of the Golden State Killer's DNA and just needed a match. When they ran it through the public database, they identified a relative of the killer and used the family tree to find their suspect. Police hope to use a similar method to finally catch the Zodiac.

Fifty years later, the police are still stumped by the Zodiac killer. Who is he? Why did he kill? Why have investigators never been able to identify him? Although police continue to track down every new lead in the case, the fact remains that the Zodiac killer may never be found.

TIMELINE

1966

- In October, Cheri Jo Bates is murdered in Riverside, California. The killing is similar to the Zodiac's later crimes, but it has not been officially connected to the Zodiac.

1968

- In December, Betty Lou Jensen and David Faraday are murdered by the Zodiac killer on Lake Herman Road outside Vallejo, California.

1969

- On July 4, Darlene Ferrin and Mike Mageau are attacked by the Zodiac in Vallejo. Ferrin dies from her injuries, but Mageau survives.
- In August, an anonymous writer sends letters and a coded message to three California newspapers. He calls himself the Zodiac and claims credit for recent murders.
- In August, high school teacher Donald Harden and his wife, Bettye, solve the Zodiac's cryptogram.
- In September, the Zodiac attacks Cecelia Shepard and Bryan Hartnell at Lake Berryessa. Shepard dies two days later, but Hartnell survives.
- On October 11, cab driver Paul Stine is murdered by the Zodiac in San Francisco, California.
- In October, the Zodiac sends a letter to the *San Francisco Chronicle* that includes a piece of Stine's bloody shirt. In the letter, he threatens to attack a school bus.
- In November, the Zodiac sends two more letters to the *San Francisco Chronicle*.

1970

- In March, Kathleen Johns and her infant daughter are abducted on the highway near Modesto, California. She escapes and later identifies her abductor as the Zodiac killer.
- The Zodiac sends several letters to the *San Francisco Chronicle*.

1971

- The Zodiac sends a letter to the *Los Angeles Times* suggesting that he was responsible for the murder of Cheri Jo Bates in Riverside.

1974

- After years of silence, the Zodiac sends several letters to the *San Francisco Chronicle*.

1992

- Arthur Leigh Allen, who is suspected by many to be the Zodiac killer, dies in Vallejo, California.

2002

- DNA testing shows that Allen is not linked to the Zodiac killings.

2018

- Police send envelopes from the Zodiac's letters to a private lab for advanced DNA testing.

ESSENTIAL FACTS

SIGNIFICANT EVENTS

- The Zodiac's killing spree starts on December 20, 1968, when he kills Betty Lou Jensen and David Faraday in Vallejo, California.
- On August 1, 1969, three San Francisco area newspapers receive the Zodiac killer's first letters. Each letter includes a portion of a cryptogram.
- On September 27, 1969, Cecelia Shepard and Bryan Hartnell are attacked by the Zodiac killer at Lake Berryessa. A few weeks later, he kills Paul Stine in San Francisco.
- The Zodiac continues to send letters to the press through 1970 and 1971. Then he goes silent for about four years. The letters resume in 1974 and then stop again. Other letters are sent in the following years, but many people believe they are hoaxes.

KEY PLAYERS

- Betty Lou Jensen and David Faraday, two teens, were killed in a brutal attack on December 20, 1968. They were the first verified victims of the Zodiac killer.
- Detective Dave Toschi, a homicide detective with the San Francisco Police Department, spent years searching for the Zodiac killer.
- Arthur Leigh Allen, a Vallejo resident and convicted child molester, was a prime suspect in the Zodiac case, but police were never able to gather enough evidence to charge him.

IMPACT ON SOCIETY

In the late 1960s, a serial killer known as the Zodiac terrorized Northern California. From his first murders, the Zodiac killer, with his taunting messages to police and the press, has fascinated people around the world. Part of the mystery involves the series of cryptograms the Zodiac sent to the press. The first one, sent in three pieces to different newspapers, contained a chilling message about how the Zodiac enjoyed killing his victims. Despite the efforts of expert and amateur codebreakers, the Zodiac's later cryptograms remain unsolved. Linked to five murders, the Zodiac claimed to have more than 30 victims. Despite numerous pieces of evidence and leads, police have never been able to uncover the identity of the Zodiac killer. The case has been the inspiration for many legends and theories, as well as a number of books, websites, and movies. All the while, the mystery of the man behind the Zodiac killer remains unsolved.

QUOTE

"For me, the Zodiac case is the number one unsolved American criminal mystery. . . . I think there are more people looking into this case than any other case."

—Mark Hewitt, a California-based author who has published a trilogy of books on the Zodiac killer

GLOSSARY

abduction
The act of taking someone without their consent.

alibi
A claim that proves an accused person could not be guilty of a crime.

anagram
A word, phrase, or name formed by rearranging the letters of another.

ballistics
The science of projectiles and firearms.

bulletin
A short official statement or broadcast of news.

caliber
The diameter of the inside of a gun barrel.

cipher
A code or disguised way of writing.

cryptogram
A coded text or message.

decipher
To convert a text written in code to plain language.

DNA
Deoxyribonucleic acid, the chemical that is the basis of genetics, through which various traits are passed from parent to child.

linguistics
The study of language and its structure.

ADDITIONAL RESOURCES

SELECTED BIBLIOGRAPHY

Fagan, Kevin. "The Zodiac Case, 50 Years Later." *San Francisco Chronicle*, 14 Dec. 2018, sfchronicle.com. Accessed 3 May 2019.

Fagan, Kevin. "Zodiac Killer Case: How the San Francisco Chronicle Was Involved." *San Francisco Chronicle*, 14 Dec. 2018, sfchronicle.com. Accessed 3 May 2019.

Graysmith, Robert. *Zodiac*. St. Martin's Marek, 1986.

FURTHER READINGS

Carmichael, L. E. *Forensic Science: In Pursuit of Justice*. Abdo, 2015.

Hunt, Amber, and Emily G. Thompson. *Unsolved Murders: True Crime Cases Uncovered*. DK, 2019.

Parks, Peggy J. *DNA Evidence and Investigation*. ReferencePoint Press, 2010.

ONLINE RESOURCES

Booklinks
NONFICTION NETWORK
FREE! ONLINE NONFICTION RESOURCES

To learn more about the Zodiac killer, please visit **abdobooklinks.com** or scan this QR code. These links are routinely monitored and updated to provide the most current information available.

MORE INFORMATION

For more information on this subject, contact or visit the following organizations:

ALCATRAZ EAST CRIME MUSEUM

2757 Parkway
Pigeon Forge, TN 37863
865-453-3278
alcatrazeast.com

The museum offers exhibits focused on famous American crimes and has a crime library that includes information online.

AMERICAN ACADEMY OF FORENSIC SCIENCES (AAFS)

410 North 21st St.
Colorado Springs, CO 80904
719-636-1100
aafs.org

The AAFS is a professional society dedicated to promoting forensic science education and improving the accuracy and precision of forensic science.

SAN FRANCISCO CHRONICLE

901 Mission St.
San Francisco, CA 94103
415-777-1111
sfchronicle.com

The *Chronicle*, San Francisco's largest newspaper, received several letters from the Zodiac killer and worked with police on efforts to identify the killer.

SOURCE NOTES

CHAPTER 1. ATTACK AT LOVERS' LANE

1. George McEvoy. "Friends Quizzed in Slaying of Teen Pair Near Vallejo." *San Francisco Sunday Examiner & Chronicle,* 22 Dec. 1968, zodiacciphers.com. Accessed 5 Aug. 2019.

2. "Mystery Motive: Police Seeking Teens' Slayer," *San Francisco Chronicle*, 23 Dec. 1968, zodiacciphers.com. Accessed 5 Aug. 2019.

CHAPTER 2. FOURTH OF JULY MURDER

1. Robert Graysmith. *Zodiac*. St. Martin's Marek, 1986. 13.

2. "Blue Rock Springs Attack 7-4-1969." *Zodiac Ciphers*, n.d., zodiacciphers.com. Accessed 5 Aug. 2019.

3. "Crime Report." *Zodiac Killer*, n.d., zodiackiller.com. Accessed 5 Aug. 2019.

4. Graysmith, *Zodiac*, 31.

5. Graysmith, *Zodiac*, 32.

6. Graysmith, *Zodiac*, 32.

CHAPTER 3. MYSTERIOUS LETTERS FROM THE KILLER

1. "*Chronicle* Envelope Front." *Zodiac Killer*, n.d., zodiackiller.com. Accessed 5 Aug. 2019.

2. "*Chronicle* Envelope Front."

3. Robert Graysmith. *Zodiac*. St. Martin's Marek, 1986. 54–55.

4. Graysmith, *Zodiac*, 55.

5. Graysmith, *Zodiac*, 56.

CHAPTER 4. A HOODED ATTACKER AT THE LAKE

1. Robert Graysmith. *Zodiac*. St. Martin's Marek, 1986. 65.

2. Graysmith, *Zodiac*, 67.

3. Graysmith, *Zodiac*, 71.

4. Graysmith, *Zodiac*, 74.

5. "Zodiac Letter 5." *History*, 2 Nov. 2017, history.com. Accessed 5 Aug. 2019.

CHAPTER 5. PRESIDIO HEIGHTS MURDER

1. Robert Graysmith. *Zodiac*. St. Martin's Marek, 1986. 84.

CHAPTER 6. MORE LETTERS FROM THE ZODIAC

1. "Zodiac Letter 6." *History*, 2 Nov. 2017, history.com. Accessed 5 Aug. 2019.

2. "Zodiac Letter 6."

3. "Zodiac Letter 6."

4. "Zodiac Letter 6."

5. Robert Graysmith. *Zodiac*. St. Martin's Marek, 1986. 119.

6. "340 Cipher." *Zodiac Killer*, n.d., zodiackiller.com. Accessed 5 Aug. 2019.

7. "Message to the Zodiac Killer." *Zodiac Ciphers*, 25 Aug. 2016, zodiacciphers.com. Accessed 5 Aug. 2019.

8. "Bomb Letter." *Zodiac Killer*, n.d., zodiackiller.com. Accessed 3 Apr. 2019.

SOURCE NOTES CONTINUED

CHAPTER 7. A HIGHWAY ABDUCTION

1. Robert Graysmith. *Zodiac*. St. Martin's Marek, 1986. 137.

2. Graysmith, *Zodiac*, 137.

CHAPTER 8. WHERE IS THE ZODIAC?

1. "Zodiac Letter 10." *History*, 2 Nov. 2017, history.com. Accessed 5 Aug. 2019.

2. "Zodiac Letter 10."

3. "Zodiac Letter 11." *History*, 2 Nov. 2017, history.com. Accessed 5 Aug. 2019.

4. "Frequently Asked Questions (FAQ)." *Zodiac Killer*, n.d., zodiackiller.com. Accessed 5 Aug. 2019.

5. "Zodiac Letter 12." *History*, 2 Nov. 2017, history.com. Accessed 5 Aug. 2019.

6. Michael Butterfield. "The Zodiac Killer: A Timeline." *History*, 8 Nov. 2017, history.com. Accessed 5 Aug. 2019.

7. "Halloween Card." *Zodiac Killer*, n.d., zodiackiller.com. Accessed 5 Aug. 2019.

8. Robert Graysmith. *Zodiac*. St. Martin's Marek, 1986. 167.

9. Graysmith, *Zodiac*, 168

10. Graysmith, *Zodiac*, 170.

11. Graysmith, *Zodiac*, 171.

12. "Frequently Asked Questions (FAQ)."

13. "The Los Angeles Times Letter." *Zodiac Ciphers*, n.d., zodiacciphers.com. Accessed 5 Aug. 2019.

14. Butterfield, "The Zodiac Killer: A Timeline."

CHAPTER 9. IDENTITY UNKNOWN

1. Daniel Uria. "50 Years After First Case, Zodiac Killer Still Haunts Bay Area Investigators." *UPI*, 20 Dec. 2018, upi.com. Accessed 5 Aug. 2019.

2. Scott Bonn. "Our Curious Fascination with Serial Killers," Psychology Today, 23 Oct. 2017. psychologytoday.com. Accessed 14. Aug. 2019.

3. Kevin Fagan. "The Zodiac Case, 50 Years Later." *San Francisco Chronicle*, 14 Dec. 2018, sfchronicle.com. Accessed 5 Aug. 2019.

4. "Zodiac." *Box Office Mojo*, n.d., boxofficemojo.com. Accessed 5 Aug. 2019.

5. "Unabomber." *FBI*, n.d., fbi.gov. Accessed April 10, 2019.

6. Michael Martinez and Dan Simon. "Louisiana Man Claims His Biological Father Was Zodiac Killer." *CNN*, 14 May 2014, cnn.com. Accessed 5 Aug. 2019.

7. Gina Kolata and Heather Murphy. "The Golden State Killer Is Tracked Through a Thicket of DNA, and Experts Shudder." *New York Times*, 27 Apr. 2018, nytimes.com. Accessed 5 Aug. 2019.

INDEX

ABOUT THE AUTHOR

Carla Mooney is a graduate of the University of Pennsylvania. Today, she writes for young people and is the author of many books for young adults and children. Mooney enjoys reading about true crime and investigations.